Supernatural Mysteries

AND OTHER TALES

ALSO BY EDWARD ROWE SNOW

Supernatural Mysteries
AND OTHER TALES

_____

BY EDWARD ROWE SNOW
Illustrated

DODD, MEAD & COMPANY · NEW YORK

ISBN: 0–396–07013–2
Library of Congress Catalog Card Number: 74–25671
Printed in the United States of America
by The Haddon Craftsmen, Inc., Scranton, Penna.

I dedicate this book to my grandmother

LUCY ANNA SNOW

a deep student of the supernatural

Introduction

Far too many writers of ghost stories, tales of witches, haunt-ings, mysticism, the supernatural and exorcism, and related subjects have a tendency to attempt to prove that their con-victions are true without the slightest doubt. I do not agree with this approach, for I believe that we should be open-minded in our discussion concerning the invisible fringe area between what we know and what we are not sure of.

For example, how many of our grandfathers and grand-mothers would accept the fact that man could land on the moon? We know it has happened, but most of our ancestors would have considered that particular hypothesis absurd.

During the lecture on things supernatural which I gave at the University of New Hampshire in 1973, I emphasized my firm conviction that we should accept the *possibility* that matters which we cannot explain or comprehend *may* be actualities.

It is my contention, and I believe it a fair one, that I should offer you the tales and traditions without sugar coating and without making an attempt to influence you one way or another on which of the stories that have come down to us should be accepted as fact.

In some chapters it has been necessary to explain more about the subject matter than in others, but in a majority of the sections of this volume the material does not need explanation and I offer it without comment.

I wish to express my gratitude to the Ventress Memorial Library, Marshfield; the Allen and the Peirce Memorial Libraries of Scituate; the Boston Athenaeum; the Boston Public Library; the Thomas Crane Public Library of Quincy; the Harvard College Library; the Bostonian Society; the Society for the Preservation of New England Antiquities; the Massachusetts Archives; the Peabody Museum; the American Antiquarian Society in Worcester; the Essex Institute; the Massachusetts Marine Historical League; the National Archives; the Boston Marine Society; the Massachusetts Historical Society; the Maine Historical Society; the Nathan Tufts Library in Weymouth; and *Yankee* Magazine.

Many individuals contributed their ability and their time in the preparation of this volume. In addition to those who seek anonymity, they include Fletcher S. Bassett, Dorothy Snow Bicknell, John Leonard Bicknell, Laura Ann Bicknell, Jack Beasley, Mary Brown, Richard Carlisle, Borden Clarke of Old Authors Farm, Frederick G. S. Clow, Frederick M. Cochrane, Arthur Cunningham, James Douglass, Walter Spahr Ehrenfeld, Nina Ehrenfeld, George M. Fallon, Leo Flaherty, Edward B. Garside, James A. Gibbs, Jr., George Gloss, Marie Hansen, John R. Herbert, Melina Herron, James Hicks, Dorothy Haegg Jacobson, Trevor Johnson, Ron Knight, Joseph Kolb, Gary P. Kosciusko, William McIntire, Walter P. McNaney, Maggie Mills, Robert E. Moody, Richard Nakashian, Joel O'Brien, Paul Prokopas, William Pyne, Elva Ruiz, Mrs. Carlton Rutledge, Helen Ryan Salkowski, Frederick J. Sanford, Grace Saphir, Alfred

K. Schroeder, William Smits, Donald B. Snow, Roy Wendell, Susan Williams, and Martin Zard.

Anna-Myrle, my wife, has truly shown her love, ability, and devotion by her help in all aspects of this volume.

I trust that you will enjoy this book.

EDWARD ROWE SNOW

Marshfield, Massachusetts

Contents

Illustrations

Following page 82

A phantom ship
Sea monster seen from the *Daedalus*
Gloucester sea serpent
Fight between sea serpent and sperm whale
A sixteenth-century sea serpent
A modern sea monster
Crowd at Mann Hill monster site
Head of the Mann Hill monster
Hydrarchos sillimani
A Norwegian sea serpent
Last sighting of Captain Herndon
The sinking of the *Central America*
Undersea salvage work, 1850s
Loss of the *Royal George*
Salvage efforts on the *Royal George,* 1783
Salvage efforts on the *Royal George,* 1841

PART 1

The Bermuda Triangle
and Other Mysteries

1

The Bermuda Triangle

At two o'clock on the afternoon of Wednesday, December 5, 1945, five United States torpedo bombers left Fort Lauderdale, Florida, on a mission which was to last less than two hours. With fourteen men aboard the five planes, the aircraft were to fly a triangular course.

Then, suddenly, radio contact was established with the Fort Lauderdale control tower. The commander of the torpedo bombers stated that he could not see land and must be off course. Unable to identify anything resembling a position, his last four words were: "Looks like we are. . . ." The five planes were never heard from again. When uninterrupted silence followed the four words, a Martin flying boat was dispatched with thirteen men aboard to investigate, but within minutes radio communications with the flying boat were lost, and that plane was never heard from again either.

Those two flights became to flyers what the loss of the ten persons aboard the *Mary Celeste* is to all of us who are interested in sea mysteries.

Reviewing the situation, we find that the operation had

been planned as a routine two-hour mission. Four of the planes carried three men each; the fifth had only two aboard, since the third crew member of that plane was unable to make the trip. Everything had been properly tested before the flight. Radios had been checked with both tower and pilot, and fuel was adequate for each plane for a sky journey of almost eleven hundred miles. Life-saving equipment was all in satisfactory order with rafts and Mae West preservers, and all engines had been given the usual stiff inspection.

The flight was to outline a so-called triangle similar to the triangular course of hurricane-watch flights out of Bermuda. As the flight progressed in the next hour and three-quarters, four routine position reports were made. All indications are that in no way did these reports reveal any unusual situation. Then, at 3:45, the control tower established contact with the flight leader, who stated that he was unable to see land. Apparently off course for some mysterious reason, he either could not understand or did not properly explain his situation.

Back in the tower at Fort Lauderdale, the operator asked the flight leader for his position. The enigmatic reply came at once. The leader stated that he was "not sure of where we are," and again reported that he could "not see land!" Ten minutes went by. Then the tower operator could hear the members of the different flight crews talking to each other. Utterly confused, the pilots were asking each other questions in tones approaching panic, resembling a group of hikers lost in mountains with which they were not familiar. Apparently the weather was clear and there seemed no reason for what was happening.

Four o'clock arrived, and a few minutes later the patrol leader handed his command over to another pilot. Under the known circumstances, this was an almost unprecedented act. At 4:25 the new leader spoke to the tower at Fort Lauderdale and stated that he also could not tell where the flight was, for he couldn't make anything out either. He estimated that the position of the five planes was about 225 miles east of the Fort Lauderdale base.

Then came the four words I have already mentioned, the last ever to be heard from any of the planes, "Looks like we are. . . ." These four words were heard clearly by the listeners at Fort Lauderdale. Constituting the last message from the five bombers out over the Atlantic, the phrase is an important one.

Commander Howard S. Roberts, executive officer of the naval air station, was in the control tower as the final four-word message came in. He ordered the rescue alarm sounded and declared a vital emergency. Soon he watched the huge Martin Mariner flying boat climb into the sky. Especially equipped for rescue work, the Mariner, with its crew of thirteen, had a reinforced hull which could land in the water in rough weather under radically adverse conditions.

Ten minutes after takeoff the Mariner pilot talked with the Fort Lauderdale tower and gave a routine radio check without any mention of trouble, but the tower lost contact immediately afterward, and the Mariner never communicated again.

By sunset that December day Coast Guard vessels and naval craft were in action, proceeding up and down the area where it was believed the last words from the planes had been sent out. As the day ended, a real "sunset calm" was present in the general area. Nevertheless, search as they might, the hunters sighted nothing at all. There were no telltale oil slicks, no flares of any type, and no floating debris in sight.

All that long night the men of the Navy and the Coast Guard continued their efforts. There were no results at all. With the coming of dawn the aircraft carrier *Solomons* entered the search. By noon more than 255 planes from the

United States, assisted by thirty-two Royal Air Force planes from the Bahamas, criss-crossed the area time and again. All had the same result—failure.

A hundred soldiers, sailors, and civilians went up and down the beaches of Florida, scouring the region for any type of debris or bodies. Nothing was found. Later, planes flew out over the Gulf of Mexico, and soon the complete search had totaled a quarter-million square miles! The entire project was one of the greatest search efforts ever carried out in America, but it ended in complete failure.*

Five days after the disaster, with all searchers called off the project, a naval board of inquiry met to establish the facts. Six planes had vanished on a clear day over the Florida Straits, and, for no reason ever determined, must have crashed into the sea. The flyers all had been indoctrinated as to what to do in case of trouble, and it seemed impossible to believe that every man was eliminated from the picture before he could do something of a tangible nature to save himself.

As the sun that day was still shining, each pilot could have reached the mainland simply by flying westward. Why was this not accomplished by even one of the six planes? If the aircraft all had disintegrated in the air, some fragment or part should have remained afloat, and from all the gas obviously still in the planes when they hit the water, some oil patches should have been observed by the scores of searchers who spent a total of hundreds of hours hunting for signs of debris. Nevertheless, not a raft, life jacket, or fragment of parachute was ever sighted. Nor did any article connected with the six planes ever wash ashore.

Airplanes and ships are said to have been affected by

---

*Some time later, on the Massachusetts south shore, a burned-out Navy flare floated in between Hen Island and Branch Creek, Marshfield. The flare has been preserved, but it was never identified.

supernatural beings, monsters, or demons from out of this world within the area of the Bermuda Triangle. It is possible that William Shakespeare himself was the originator of the idea. In his *Tempest,* probably his last play, the bard unquestionably locates his "uninhabited island" at Bermuda.* Shakespeare on at least three occasions comes very close to William Strachey's ideas.

Strachey's *A True Repertory of the Wrack* was not published until after Shakespeare's death, but Shakespeare had access to the manuscript. Indeed, Strachey mentions that Bermuda is a place "terrible to all that ever touched on them." The Devil's Islands were feared and avoided by all superstitious travelers of the period above any other place in the world!

Many believed and others still believe that demons and devils once guided ships to their destruction, and that in today's modern world they send airplanes to their doom. There are those who say that the North Rocks of Bermuda stand for all that is mystical and supernatural in the area. In 1948 I flew out to them for the first time and came under the spell of the particularly impressive coral boulder which dominates the area. Standing sixty feet high above the sea and the other reefs in that region, North Rock is about twelve miles out from the mainland of Bermuda.

The design of the seal of the Bermuda Company shows the wreck of the *Bonaventura* outlined against North Rock, thus emphasizing the reefs and rocks as treacherous areas for ships.

In 1876 an adventurous photographer, James B. Heyl, journeyed to North Rock. Those were the days of the cumbersome photographic wet plate,** but in spite of his hard-

*See my *Incredible Mysteries and Legends of the Sea,* pages 236, 237.
**See my *Fantastic Folklore and Fact,* page 105, for the story of the first aerial picture ever made anywhere, that over Boston in 1860.

ships Heyl made an outstanding picture of the well-known massive rock. Although it was necessary to set up the tripod on the coral reef in shallow water which was constantly lapping at Heyl's feet and the plates had to be developed as soon as they were exposed, the photographer came back to Bermuda in triumph.

When I visited Gibb's Hill Light at Bermuda in 1948, I stood on the lookout platform of the lighthouse to watch the last smoke disappear from the steamship *Fort Amherst*, which had left Hamilton some hours before. At the time of my visit the lighthouse keeper suggested that I investigate the story of the training ship *Atalanta*, because what he had been told constituted a strange, unsolvable mystery.

As I discovered and mentioned elsewhere in this book, in January 1880, Captain Francis Stirling sailed the frigate *Atalanta* away from Bermuda's sunny islands, bound for England with three hundred young men training for the sea. Nothing has been heard from the *Atalanta* since that time. Even today when the Bermuda Triangle is discussed, the *Atalanta* is often mentioned.

There may be some vast, terrible "something" which has made this part of the world at times particularly vulnerable to the ominous and sinister.

More than a generation ago the 59th Weather Reconnaissance Squadron, popularly known as the Hurricane Hunters, began flying a triangular route out of Bermuda's Kindley Field* on weather missions. Gradually, researchers who studied unexplained aircraft disasters and enigmatic shipping tragedies began to use the already coined term "Bermuda Triangle" to include the area where these disasters occurred.

*Named for Captain Field E. Kindley, American World War I flight commander.

In addition to the loss of the *Atalanta* in 1880 and the six planes in 1945, there are scores upon scores of other unexplained disasters. The strangest is that of the awesome schooner of skeletons, the *Eliza Ann*, which drifted into Ely's Harbor in December 1883. Because of intensive research in Boston and at Ely's Harbor in Bermuda, I was able to solve part of the weird story of the skeleton schooner, and recorded my findings in *Great Atlantic Adventures*.

Sailing from Boston on December 11, 1832, the *Eliza Ann* vanished almost as soon as she was hull down beyond Boston Light, only to be found adrift off Bermuda with everyone dead aboard on December 27, 1833. When discovered, the *Eliza Ann* was a veritable ship of skeletons.

Through the years other incidents of similar nature have made the Bermuda Triangle an area to be considered carefully in any summary of Atlantic mysteries. In March 1866, fourteen years before the *Atalanta* vanished in 1880, the bark *Lotta* disappeared off the north coast of Haiti. She had been called a mystery craft for several years before, having participated in a weird piratical mission which forever afterward proved to be an enigma to the Bermuda authorities.

Then in 1918, after eleven other vessels had mysteriously vanished in a short period of time, the loss of the U.S.S. *Cyclops* claimed the headlines. Many explanations were given as to why she vanished, but no one ever offered one that was satisfactory.*

The *Marine Sulphur Queen* disappeared at sea February 3, 1963, in the dreaded Bermuda Triangle. Thirty-nine men vanished and only one life ring and life jacket, evidently knotted together by a man's shirt, could ever be connected with the disaster which befell the ship.

It is probable that more than one hundred craft of various

*See my *Fury of the Seas*, pages 215–220.

types have disappeared mysteriously in the Bermuda Triangle. It is true that many experts, although publicly disclaiming any belief in mysterious objects or forces, have privately admitted that there may be something more than human error involved.

One answer may be that gigantic waves form for reasons never really explained or even understood. Around the year 1938 the United States Navy was so impressed by the recording of so many mysterious disappearances that they investigated the situation. Studying unusual waves observed and endured at sea and on shore, they hoped to come up with the right answer. Those researching the subject wrote to me asking if I would send them one of my storm pictures of Minot's Light being battered by the sea. I mailed them my photo of the so-called Ermine Wrap Light, which I took at the height of a storm in a circling airplane.* The resulting government book contained much of various ocean phenomena. It was called *Wind, Waves at Sea, Breakers and Surf* and was published in 1947.

Henry B. Bigelow and W. T. Edmonson, who wrote the book mentioned above, tell of unusual waves which have risen to heights of well over one hundred feet. The record wave, estimated by the commanding officer of the U.S.S. *Ramapo,* reached 112 feet.

Extreme height of waves usually cannot be blamed for the loss of planes which vanished, but for two Tudor IV British planes, the *Star Tiger* and the *Star Ariel,* which had to land in the sea, high waves could indeed be a factor in their disappearance.

On Friday, January 30, 1948, the *Star Tiger,* a four-engine

*The "Ermine Wrap" photograph, which was published in *Life* magazine, was taken from the air on November 26, 1939. It is not the same picture I made some years later which Time-Life's book *The Sea* now includes.

Tudor IV with twenty-five passengers aboard, was on the way from Santa Maria in the Azores to Hamilton, Bermuda. Pilot David Colby had radioed at 10:30 the night before that he would reach Hamilton an hour and a half late, or around one o'clock in the morning. Then, about 1:00 A.M., Colby sent out another message: "Still approximately 440 miles northeast of Bermuda. Bucking strong head winds." That was the last message ever received, for the *Star Tiger* was never heard from again.

Aboard the plane were Air Marshall Sir Arthur Coningham, who commanded the Second Tactical Air Force of the Allies during the invasion of Normandy, and British Treasury Assistant Secretary Ernest Brooks.

The usual efforts were made to establish radio contact, but they brought no success, and air–sea rescue planes were sent out.

It was believed that Colby was able to ditch the plane without serious damage. The Tudor IV, if she had landed successfully, should have floated until the passengers and crew had the time to clamber aboard the rubber life rafts. Not only was the water fairly warm—at least sixty degrees—but the survival kits included a small hand-cranked radio operated on the 500-kilocycles band. Any plane flying within fifty miles of the rubber raft with the radio working should have been able to hear from a survivor.

Colonel Thomas D. Ferguson, commander of the United States air force base in Bermuda, sent out two Flying Fortresses from Kindley Field, Bermuda, to search for the missing craft. Another B-17 took off from MacDill Field, Florida. All three carried the latest lifeboats, which could be dropped by parachute. Mitchell Field, New York, sent out an army transport with orders to patrol from New Jersey to Long Island, as far out as 550 miles from shore.

Three Coast Guard cutters, the *Mendota,* the *Cherokee,*

and the *Androscoggin,* went to sea under orders of the New York Eastern Area Search and Rescue Headquarters, while two steamers covered a triangle between Bermuda, a point four hundred miles due north, and another point three hundred miles northeast. No fewer than fourteen planes of the Air Transport Command took to the air to aid in the search.

Pan American ordered its planes to fly over the area in which it was believed the Tudor IV was lost, but bad weather set in and visibility was very poor. Newfoundland and San Juan, Puerto Rico, also sent planes into the area.

As the sun went down on the first day of the gigantic hunt, Colonel Ferguson, at Search Command Headquarters, reported the weather had now become so unfavorable that all planes would have to be grounded, for surface waves were building as high as forty feet.

The steamer *Troubadour* then reported that she had sighted a "low-flying plane between Bermuda and Delaware," but later a Pan American plane announced she was the aircraft sighted and had not been in trouble.

A flyer from Westover Field, Massachusetts, sighted a round object in the water with black and yellow boxes in the immediate vicinity.

Then a search plane pilot noticed oil slicks 250 miles northwest of Bermuda, while another plane five hundred miles east-northeast of Bermuda also sighted slicks, with more slicks reported less than one hundred miles northeast of Bermuda. Search and Rescue Headquarters said the slicks described were probably caused by bilges pumped out by passing steamers.

Two planes reported a raft with flares to the south of Bermuda. The tanker *Esso Philadelphia* picked up the raft, but it had been in the water for months and possibly years.

A public inquiry was then begun in England into the loss of the *Star Tiger.* G. S. Lindgren of the British Ministry stated that all Tudor IV's would be withdrawn from service until investigations were carried out.

The aircraft continued to search, and in all forty planes flew more than 220,000 square miles around Bermuda. Hope faded rapidly and soon it was realized that all aboard the *Star Tiger* were lost.

Radio operators in various areas claim that code messages revealed the names *Tiger* and *Star Tiger*. On February 3, late at night, officers at Halifax Air Force Headquarters heard amateur tappings of a strange nature. No tappings were heard in the daytime, however. The Federal Communications Commission attempted triangular fixing, but failed. Forty-three aircraft were alerted, and ships everywhere stood by for instructions. The hours passed, and then the days, but no more tappings were ever heard. Possibly an amateur with a twisted mind instigated the tappings and then, afraid of the consequences were a triangular fix to catch him, stayed off the air.

The British Ministry of Civil Aviation announced in London that it was "presumed" that the plane with its passengers and crew had been lost at sea.

John Wallace Spencer in his *Limbo of the Lost* tells us that on September 28, 1948, the verdict of the court appointed by the minister of civil aviation to investigate the disappearance of the *Star Tiger* was published as a white paper.

The fate of the *Star Tiger*, must remain an unsolved mystery. "It may truly be said that no more baffling problem has ever been presented for investigation," was the statement of the court. Of course, the possibility of a bomb explosion always exists in any passenger flight.

The design of the Tudor IV aircraft, as far as could be ascertained, did not cause the mishap. There were possible "technical errors or omissions." It is improbable that fire broke out or that a disastrous mechanical breakdown or any part of the plane's power plant caused the trouble.

The report terminates by stating that in the "complete absence of any reliable evidence as to either the nature or the cause of the disaster to the *Star Tiger,* the court has not been able to do more than suggest possibilities, none of which reaches the level even of probability. What happened in this case will never be known."

About a year after the *Star Tiger* vanished, another of the Tudor planes, the *Star Ariel,* disappeared without a trace on its way from Bermuda to Kingston, Jamaica. The two mysterious losses, coming as they did a year apart, not only caused the immediate withdrawal of the Tudor aircraft from passenger service, but also strengthened belief in the legend of the Bermuda Triangle.

No one has ever been able to give a satisfactory explanation for the disappearance of the *Star Ariel,* which vanished while flying in perfect weather on January 17, 1949. Dozens of aircraft flew a million unsucrnessful miles in a search covering more than fifty thousand square miles of sea. Not a trace of the plane was ever found. After a long hearing and investigation, a statement was issued that "the cause of the accident is unknown."

Some experts have ruled out the theory that the plane exploded in mid-air while flying at eighteen thousand feet. At that height the pilot might have been able to radio a Mayday.

The commonplace messages sent by the crew of *Star Ariel* shortly after leaving Bermuda offer no clues. The first, to Kingston, stated that the plane had taken off from Bermuda at 8:41 A.M. and would arrive in Kingston in six hours. By then it had flown out of the 150-mile-radius control area of Bermuda and asked Kingston to accept flight control. Barely seven minutes later the last message ever heard from the aircraft was sent:

I was over 30 degrees N at 1337 hrs (GMT) [9:37 A.M.]
I am changing frequency to MRX. [frequency 6523 kcs]

The message was acknowledged, which gave the plane's
thirty-one-year-old pilot, Captain J. C. McPhee, the authority to change clearance to Kingston.

A strange part of the incident is that incredible time wait
—a full four hours and fifteen minutes—before anyone
started wondering about the plane's whereabouts. There was
no interest shown until 1:52 in the afternoon. Then Kingston
contacted Bermuda asking about the *Star Ariel,* which
should have been only one hour out of Kingston. Blame was
later placed on Kingston for ignoring the plane for so long.

Message after message flashed back and forth across the
sky between Kingston, Bermuda, and the United States. A
massive air–sea search was launched which lasted five days.
Flying practically within sight of each other at all times,
planes combed almost every inch of over fifty-five thousand
square miles of sea between Bermuda, Kingston, and the
U.S. mainland. An armada of ships from every interested
country also joined in the search, including an ocean going
tug, *Foundation Lillian,* then stationed in Bermuda. But no
wreckage, no bodies, not even an oil slick were ever found.

Indeed, the Bermuda Triangle, a vast expanse of sea covering almost half a million miles, has long been a source of fear,
speculation, and superstition. There are those who call it the
"Twilight Zone for ships and planes." In any case, this incredible part of the Atlantic has been the scene of more
enigmatic tragedies of sea and air than any other area.

If we study the total of disasters in the Triangle, we find
them far out of proportion to more heavily traveled sea and
sky areas. More than twenty ships and aircraft and over one
thousand people have disappeared there since World War II
began. None of the disappearances suggests logical, natural

explanations. Weird disappearances in the Bermuda Triangle area go back to earliest times, although the first mariner to visit there, Christopher Columbus, did make it successfully, but not without incident, as we shall report later in this narrative.

In the old days there were tales of sea monsters, giant octopi, squid, and devils waiting to overwhelm galleons and crews. Today we do not believe that monsters and devils are responsible, but many ardent flying-saucer devotees blame people from outer space. Some of them state that the Triangle may be a sort of "collecting basin of human specimens" which are then removed to "other worlds."

While in Bermuda several years ago I was told that one enthusiast believes there are in fact six such areas—three in the northern hemisphere and three in the southern hemisphere of the globe. The Bermuda Triangle reaches to central Florida and Puerto Rico and extends from about 30–40° north latitude and from about 55–85°W. Another area lies some 250 miles south of the Japanese island of Honshu and is in the general longitude of 140°E. Still another zone exists in the Mediterranean Sea, which is an oval-shaped area. The three mystery triangles below the equator which greatly resemble the shape, size, and position of those in the north are near South America, South Africa, and Australia. Each is said to be about 40° of latitude south and about 35° wide.

When Columbus sailed through both the Sargasso Sea and Bermuda Triangle area on his discovery voyage to San Salvador Island in the Bahamas on September 15, 1492, he recorded seeing what he then described as "a remarkable bolt of fire" falling into the sea. Later he reported that his men were terrified by a baffling disturbance of the ship's compass. Thus, an air of mystery was given to the Bermuda Triangle by its first known navigator.

Four American naval ships vanished without explanation

in the triangle between 1781 and 1812. But it was in wartime in 1918 that the legend of the Bermuda Triangle really began. In that year an American Navy ship—the U.S.S. *Cyclops*—set out from Brazil to the United States with a cargo of manganese. Aboard were a crew of 213 and sixty-seven passengers. The *Cyclops* called at Barbados in the British West Indies to take on fuel and provisions. It was a fair March day when the ship sailed northward into the open sea. It never was heard from again.

A massive search failed to find a single clue to its disappearance, and the loss still perplexes the Navy. Recently, however, a Navy spokesman pointed out a little-known fact which might be significant. The *Cyclops* carried a contingent of hardened, court-martialed seamen being returned to the United States for imprisonment.

In 1963 an American merchant ship, two fishing boats, and two Air Force jets disappeared in the Triangle. In none of the cases did there seem to be a common natural cause to explain the disappearances. There was no unusual indication of violent air turbulence, heavy seas, magnetic storms, water spouts, or meteorites. There was an utter lack of clues to explain the fate of the ships and aircraft.

The Navy's official point of view is that the disappearances were strange coincidences. The Navy does not believe that any twilight zone exists where supernatural forces destroy ships and planes. But even the Navy must admit there is such a possibility.

2

Mystery of the *Atalanta*

Scores upon scores of hurricanes have battered the shores of Bermuda, bringing death and misery to many of the inhabitants of that land seven hundred miles off the shores of the United States. One incident, however, cannot be attributed to any of the great gales or hurricanes, and that is the utter vanishing of the British training ship *Atalanta* almost a century ago from the waters between Bermuda and the British Isles. No storm of any intensity hit the area at the time; in fact, for a long period the weather was unusually calm.

In January 1880, Captain Francis Stirling sailed the frigate *Atalanta* away from Bermuda's sunny islands, bound for England with three hundred young men training for the sea. Nothing has been heard from the *Atalanta* since.

While in Bermuda, Captain Stirling had written a letter to his wife in Swansea, Wales, to the effect that he planned to arrive at Spithead about March 1, and another officer conveyed the same message to a friend in Portsmouth.

Although the weeks went by and the training ship failed to appear, no one in England seemed particularly anxious about it. The very nature of the voyage, after all, was to give the young seamen training on the ocean. A few weeks did not matter one way or another. But when the papers announced that the *Atalanta* was considered overdue, the people became concerned. A majority of the boys came from Portsmouth and Devonport, and little else was talked about in those two towns for many months afterward. Each little fragment of rumor or gossip was important to the parents of those aboard the *Atalanta*.

The first unfavorable report came from the gunboat *Avon*, which had sighted masses of wreckage from an unidentified vessel off the Azores, close to the usual route of the training ships. Nothing was discovered in the water bearing the *Atalanta*'s name, however, and there was little chance of learning whether or not she was the lost ship.

Some people erroneously thought that the *Atalanta*, formerly the *Juno*, was a sister ship of the *Eurydice*, which had foundered in 1878. Consequently, they considered that the *Atalanta*'s reserve of buoyancy had been assured by shortening the masts of the training ship six feet to prevent a recurrence of the *Eurydice*'s disaster.

Another supposition concerned ballast. Captain Stirling had been furnished with stability figures for the ship, which varied according to the changing position of the load line. A story was circulated that when the fresh-water tanks had emptied, he had failed to refill them with salt water for ballast, but this theory was scoffed at by the experts, who claimed that Captain Stirling would not have made such an omission.*

Shortly after the ship was overdue, Thomas Brassery, a

*Possibly not, but the officer in charge of filling the fuel tanks on the *Andrea Doria* with salt water did not carry out his important task, and the *Andrea Doria* sank.

noted mariner and nautical expert, expressed the opinion that the *Atalanta* had probably been delayed by a gale and might have been damaged to some extent. He thought, however, that she was still afloat and would soon be reported.

On April 21, 1880, the London *Times* published a letter from Admiral B. J. Sullivan of Bournemouth:

April 19, 1880

To the Editor of the *Times*
Sir,—

Will you allow me through the *Times* to correct an erroneous impression respecting the *Atalanta?* She has been called "a sister ship to the *Eurydice,*" but the truth is they are totally different. . . .

Like the sloop class of Sir W. Symonds, his small frigates were the stiffest vessels under stiff sail we ever possessed; so much so that he would not allow them at first more than 5 tons of ballast, instead of from 30 to 60 tons, which old class ships would have had.

I only mention these facts to show that in choosing a ship of that class as a training ship, the Admiralty could not possibly have made a safer choice. . . .

The one danger that no human can guard against is floating wrecks, or dismantled hulls of forsaken ships, which could not be seen on dark nights.

I am, Sir, your obedient servant,
B. J. Sullivan, Admiral

Finally, six vessels from the Channel Fleet were sent out in search of the *Atalanta,* sailing abreast several miles apart in a wide path across the sea. They could not find the slightest trace of the missing frigate. One of the ships returned in May with the sad news that there was absolutely nothing to report.

Late in June a message was sent from Nova Scotia that a barrel stave had been picked up near Halifax with a penciled inscription:

Atalanta going down April 12, 1880. No hope. Send this to Mrs. Mary White, Piers, Sussex. James White.

Shortly afterward, a bottle with a note was found on the shores of an unidentified Massachusetts town. Neither of the messages was accepted as genuine, however.

On April 20, 1880, the H.M.S. *Wye* left Gibraltar to search for the *Atalanta,* and on the twenty-fourth day of the same month came upon a small boat. In the craft was an old man, alive but too feeble to speak. At the ship's hospital, he died without ever uttering a word despite all possible care. With thoughts of the missing *Atalanta* fresh in the minds of all, word quickly spread that a survivor from the *Atalanta* had been rescued by the *Wye,* only to die aboard without speaking a single syllable. After many months, however, it was decided that the old man had probably been a fisherman separated from his vessel in the fog.

So, we are faced with one of the great mysteries of the Atlantic Ocean. As Joseph Conrad wrote so aptly many years ago, the ocean has remained "the irreconcilable enemy of ships and men ever since ship and men had the unheard-of audacity to go afloat together in the face of his frown." And to that irreconcilable enemy we must, with the *Atalanta,* charge off another beautiful ship.

3

Lithobolia

Being an Exact and True Account (by way of Journal) of the various actions of infernal Spirits, or *Devils Incarnate* Witches, or both; and the great Disturbance and Amazement they gave to *George Waltons* Family, at a place called *Great Island,* in the Province of *New Hantshire* in New England, chiefly in throwing about (by an Invisible Hand) *Stones, Bricks* and *Brick-bats* of all Sizes, with several other things, as *Hammers, Mauls, Iron-Crows, Spits,* and other domestick Utensils, as came into their Hellish Minds, and this for the space of a Quarter of a Year. By R. C., Esq., who was a sojourner in the same Family the whole Time, and an Ocular Witness of those Diabolick Inventions. The Contents hereof being manifestly known to the Inhabitants of that Province, and Persons of other Provinces, and is upon record in his Majestie's Council Court held for that Province. 4to. Dedication 2, and pp. 16. London: Printed and are to be sold by *E. Whitlook* near *Stationers-Hall,* 1698.

The above title page was my introduction in 1942 to a small pamphlet called *Lithobolia.* I was then in London, on duty with the Eighth Air Force. Anxious to examine this strange booklet, as I had been told it concerned one of the weirdest New England stories on record, I was disappointed when informed that because of the air raids all of the rare library books had been moved out of London. Later, when I transferred to the 12th Bomber Command to participate in the African invasion, I left London without having seen more than a copy of the title of the book, but since then I have been able to read it.

Broadsides, pamphlets, and booklets of former centuries fascinate me, and I've often quoted from manuscripts of long ago. The broadside *Threnodia,* telling of a shipwreck off Scituate, Massachusetts, in 1693, is one of these ancient, fascinating publications. Morton of Merrymount in his *New England Canaan* gives us the story of hanging by proxy, while *More Wonders of the Invisible World,* written by Robert Calef (in the same year that Collamore, the subject of *Threnodia,* was drowned off Scituate), is outstanding.

Lithobolia was printed at London in 1698 and covers the experience of the Walton family of Great Island, New Hampshire.

It is the story of the Stone-Throwing Devil of the New Hampshire coast, a narrative written by an eyewitness to the affair, Richard Chamberline, who signed his sixteen-page effort with the initials R.C. The volume is extremely rare. In the *Wonderful Providences* of Increase Mather there is an abridged version of *Lithobolia,* while a complete copy was reprinted in the *Historical Magazine* over a century ago.

George Walton, the principal character in *Lithobolia,* lived in Portsmouth in the year 1682. He had incurred the hatred of an old woman of the neighborhood by taking from her a strip of land to which she laid claim. She was said to be a witch and was believed to be at the bottom of all the mischief that subsequently drove the Walton family to the brink of despair. This old lady had in fact told Walton that he would never peacefully enjoy the land he had taken from her.

Without warning, one still Sabbath night in June, a shower of stones rattled against the sides and roof of Walton's house, as unexpected as a summer hailstorm. As soon as the stone shower ended, the residents, who were in bed, hurriedly dressed and went out to see if they could find out who had been disturbing the peace and quiet of the family. It was then ten o'clock and a bright moonlit night. The family found that the gate had been taken off the hinges and carried some distance from the house, but nothing could be seen or heard of the stone throwers.

While the family was outdoors in the moonlight, a second volley of stones whistled about their heads, driving them back into the shelter of the porch. The stones began to hit them there, however, and they quickly retreated inside, where, having bolted and barred all the doors, they awaited breathlessly the next assault of their assailants. Some of the family had been struck by the missiles, and all were thoroughly frightened.

A short time later the spectral stone shower began again, filling the room itself with flying objects which crashed through the windows to scatter the glass in every direction. Smashing down inside the chimney, the stones bounded and rebounded along the floor, while the family looked on in helpless amazement at what threatened to demolish the house over their heads. This bombardment continued intermittently for four hours.

While the stone shower kept up, Walton paced the floor of his room in great distress. Suddenly, a sledge hammer crashed through the ceiling, narrowly missing his head, and fell at his feet, making a gash in the oaken floor. At the same moment the candles were swept off the table, leaving him in total darkness.

All evidence convinced the family beyond any doubt that the stones were hurled by demon hands. In the first place, some of those which were picked up were found to be hot, as if they had just been taken out of the fire. Secondly, even though several of them had been marked, counted, and put on a table, these same stones afterward would be found flying around the room again as soon as whoever had put them down had turned his back. Thirdly, the leaden crossbars of the windows were found to be bent out and not in, showing that the stones came from inside the house. Finally, some of the girls in the family, while standing outside their home, had been terribly frightened upon seeing a hand thrust out of a window. To their certain knowledge there was no one in the room from which it came.

After Walton went to bed, though not to sleep, a heavy stone came crashing through his chamber door. He got up and locked the stone in his closet. He went back to bed, but the stone was evidently taken out by invisible hands and carried with a great noise into the next room. At this moment the spit flew up the chimney and came down again without any visible human agency involved.

This queer activity continued from day to day with only an occasional respite. Wherever the master of the house showed himself—in the barn, the field, or elsewhere, by day or by night—he was sure to receive a volley. No one who witnessed this phenomenon doubted for a moment that all these acts proceeded from the malevolence of a witch.

Unusual to a high degree were some of the pranks of the demon. Walton had a guest staying with him, Richard Chamberline, who became the faithful recorder of what happened while the storm of stones continued to rain down upon the dwelling.

One night, in order to soothe his mind, Chamberline took

up a musical instrument and began to play. Immediately "a good big stone" appeared to join in with a dance while the player looked on in amazement.

Among other tricks performed by the mischievous spirit who had taken up its unwelcome residence among the family was that of moving a cheese from the press and crumbling it over the floor. The iron used in the press was later found driven into the wall, and a kettle hung upon it. Several cocks of hay that had been mowed near the house were adroitly hung upon trees nearby, and bunches of it were twisted into wisps which were stuck up all about the house kitchen.

The narrator of all these unaccountable doings admits that certain skeptical persons persisted in believing that any or all of them might have been the deeds of human beings; but the man who wrote this story 275 years ago left no doubt about his conviction that a spirit was at work.

A direct quote from *Lithobolia* follows:

After this we were pretty quiet, saving now and then a few stones march'd about for exercise, and to keep (as it were) the Diabolical hand in use, till July 28, being Friday, when about 40 stones flew about, abroad, and in the house and Orchard, and among the trees therein, and a window broke before, was broke again, and one Room where they never used before.

August 1. On Wednesday the window in my ante-chamber was broke again, and many stones were plaid about, abroad, and in the house, in the daytime, and at night. The same day in the morning they tried this experiment; they did set on the fire a pot of Urine, and cooked pins in it, with design to have it boil, and by that means to give punishment to the witch or wizard, (that might be the wicked Procurer or Contriver of this stone affliction) and take off their own; as they had been advised. This was the effect of it:

As the liquor began to grow hot, a stone came and broke the top or mouth of it, and threw it down, and spilt what was in it; which being made good again, another stone, as the pot grew hot again, broke the handle off; and being recruited and fill'd the third time, was then with a third stone quite broke to pieces and split, and so the operation became frustrate and fruitless.

On Friday, the 4th, the fence against Mr. Walton's neighbour's door, (the woman of whom formerly there was great suspicion, and thereupon examination had, as appears upon record;) this fence being maliciously pull'd down to let their cattle into his ground; he and his servants were pelted and with about 40 stones as they went to put it up again; for she had often threatened that he should never enjoy his house and land.

Mr. Walton was hit divers times, and all that day in the field, as they were Reaping, it ceas'd not, and their fell (by the men's computation) above an hundred stones.

A woman helping to reap (among the rest) was hit 9 or 10 times, and hurt to that degree, that her left arm, hip, thigh, and leg were black and blue therewith; which she showed to the woman, Mrs. Walton, and others. Mr. Woodbridge, a divine, coming to give me a visit, was hit about the hip, and one Mr. Jeffreys a Merchant, who was with him, on the leg. A window in the kitchin that had been much batter'd before, was now quite broke out, and unwindow'd, no glass or lead at all being left: a Glass Bottle broke to pieces, and the Pewter dishes (about 9 of them) thrown down, and bent.

On Sunday, being the 6th, there fell nothing considerable, nor on Monday, (7th) save only one of the children hit with a stone on the Back. We were quiet to Tuesday the 8th. But on Wednesday (9th) above 100 stones (as they verily thought) repeated the Reapers disquiet in the corn-field, whereof some were affirm'd by Mr. Walton to be great ones indeed, near as big as a man's head; and Mrs. Walton, his Wife, being by curiosity led thither, with Intent also to make some discovery by the most diligent and vigilant Observation she could use, to obviate the idle Incredulity some inconsiderate Persons might irrationally entertain concerning this venefical* Operation; or at least to confirm her own sentiments and Belief of it. Which she did, but to her cost; for she Received an untoward Blow (with a stone) on her shoulder. There were likewise two sickles bent, crack'd and disabled with them, beating them violently out of their hands that held them; and this reiterated three times successively.

After this we injoy'd our former peace and quiet, unmolested by these stony Disturbances, that whole month of August, excepting some few times; and the last of all in the month of September, (the beginning thereof) wherein Mr. Walton himself only (the Original perhaps of this strange Adventure, as has been declared) was the designed concluding sufferer; who going in his Canoe (or Boat) from the Great Island, where he dwelt, to Portsmouth, to attend the Council, who had taken Cognizance of this matter, he being summoned thither, in order to his and the Suspect's Examination, and the Courts taking order thereabout, he was sadly hit with three pebble stones as big as ones fist; one of which broke his head, which I saw him show to the President of the Council; the others gave him that Pain on the Back, of which (with other like strokes) he complained then, and afterward to his death.

*poisonous

Richard Chamberline was anxious to have proof that his fantastic story was true. Therefore he had "Some Persons of note," who were then in the area, sign the document below as "substantial witnesses of the same stonery":

These Persons underwritten do hereby attest the truth of their being Eye-witnesses of at least half a score stones that evening thrown invisibly into the field, and in the entry of the House, Hall, and one of the chambers of George Walton's, viz:

Samuel Jennings, Esq; Governor of West Jarsey
Walter Clark, Esq; Deputy-Governor of Road-Island
Mr. Arthur Cook
Mr. Matt, Borden of Road-Island
Mr. Oliver Hooton of Barbados, Merchant
Mr. T. Maul of Salem in New England, Merchant
Captain Walter Barefoot
Mr. John Hussey
And the wife of the said Mr. Hussey.

4

The Amherst Ghost

What constitutes a ghost? Writer Elliott O'Donnell of Bristol, England, with whom I talked more than thirty years ago, told me that hauntings by real ghosts "are few and far between," but explained that no matter how few they may be, to know that they exist at all is "an untold blessing." William Oliver Stevens said that if we took the ghost seriously enough to study him, in time he might lend a hand to pull the world back to spiritual truth.

One day in 1947 I began to explore the largest cemetery in Brockton, Massachusetts, looking for the grave of a lady who played a leading part in the remarkable Amherst enigma. When the lady lived in the Brockton area, she was known as Esther Cox Shanahan and was believed to have moved to New England from Nova Scotia shortly after the turn of the present century. I was told that she had died in 1912, but that is all I ever learned. My search in that particular Brockton cemetery, and later in many others, ended in complete failure.

I first heard of Esther Cox Shanahan from the lips of

Frederick L. Blair, who was vitally concerned in another great Nova Scotia mystery, the Oak Island treasure. When Frederick Blair gave me the details of what he remembered about Mrs. Shanahan, I asked him to go over with me to Princess Street in Amherst, Nova Scotia. Mr. Blair and I walked around the vacant lot where once stood the home of Mr. and Mrs. Daniel Teed. After the excitement concerning this residence had died down, the house had been first moved and then destroyed. As far as is known, no one has ever had the courage to put another residence in that location. We examined the ruins of the cellar and the general contours of the walls, which were still indicated in the grass. In the building that once stood there one of the most remarkable events in Nova Scotian history took place.

The Amherst ghost story is an account of a home completely disrupted by a being that revealed itself through many physical manifestations, allegedly observed by scores of persons.

In the summer of 1878 eight people were living at the home of Mr. and Mrs. Daniel Teed on Princess Street. Located near the corner of Church Street, the building was a neat, two-story cottage painted yellow. There were four rooms on the first floor: parlor, dining room, sewing room, and kitchen. A pantry opened into the dining room, and the doors of the dining room and parlor opened into a hallway leading to the front door.

Should you enter the front door, you would see the stairway in the hall leading to the floor above, and after climbing the stairs, you would turn to the left on the second floor. Here the entry ran at right angles to the one on the floor below. In the center of the ceiling was a trap door, without a ladder, which led to the loft above. Surrounding the entry were four small bedrooms, each of which had a conventional door and window but no communication between. Two of the bedrooms faced the front of the house and Princess Street; the other two looked toward the stable in back.

Daniel Teed, the master of the house, was a happy, normal person with nothing to distinguish him in any way. His wife, Olive, was a good woman, and they had two children, five-year-old Willie and seventeen-month-old George.

Jane and Esther Cox, Olive's two sisters, boarded with them. Jane (or Jennie, as she was often called) was twenty-two years old and quite a beauty. Her hair was light brown and fell almost to her knees when not done up. She had a host of admirers of both sexes. Esther was short and stout and had cropped dark brown hair. Her eyes were large and gray, with a bluish tinge. She was considered a tomboy. Esther and Jennie shared a room in the front of the house with a window directly over the front door.

Two other boarders lived with the family: John Teed, Daniel's brother, and William Cox, the brother of Mrs. Teed.

Into this pleasant household *something* came. To this day the people of Nova Scotia cannot agree what that *something* was, but it all began after supper one damp, foggy September night. Nineteen-year-old Esther was already in bed when Jennie came into the room at about quarter of nine. Getting into bed, Jennie noticed that she had left the light on, so she arose and put it out and then returned to the bed in which her sister was already asleep. She bumped her head against the bedpost in the dark, and, as she did so, Esther muttered in her sleep, asking if it were not the fourth of September. Jennie agreed that it was. Suddenly Esther gave a scream and jumped out of bed, shouting that there was a mouse in the mattress. Though they searched carefully, they couldn't find the mouse and went to bed again.

The next night Esther was again certain that there was a mouse in the mattress, and when the girls began to search for it, a surprising thing happened. A pasteboard box under the bed suddenly jumped into the air and fell over on its side. Esther and Jennie agreed not to talk about it, got into bed, and fell asleep.

The next night the strange manifestations started in real earnest. Poor Esther began to balloon in size; her body actually grew larger and larger, and she screamed in pain, fearing that she would burst! Suddenly a loud report shook the room. Three more reports were heard, like peals of thunder, and then Esther shrank back to normal size and entered a state of calm repose.

Four nights later Esther had another attack but jumped into bed with Jennie before it became serious. Then all the bedclothes flew off the bed and settled in a confused heap in a far corner of the room. Mrs. Teed rushed into the room and picked up the bedclothes, placing them on the terrified girls. Again they flew off and landed on the floor. When John Teed entered the room, the pillow under Esther's head slid out, flew through the air, and hit Teed squarely in the face. A short time later two more reports were heard coming from under the bed, and then the room returned to normal.

Dr. Carritte, the family physician, was called and arrived the following evening. Esther was already in bed. Suddenly, almost the entire pillow came out from under her head and then went back to its original position. When it came out again John Teed grabbed it, but it pulled from his hands and went back under Esther's head, seemingly without human help.

Dr. Carritte stood up. "How wonderful that is!" he exclaimed, and just then the loud thunderous reports began again. Dr. Carritte looked under the bed but found nothing. He walked away, and the loud reports or explosions followed him. Just then the bedclothes flew up into the air, and before they could be replaced, everyone present heard a metallic sound, and writing appeared on the wall of the room. They read in horror the words: "ESTHER COX, YOU ARE MINE TO KILL!"

Day after day the strange events continued to take place. Dr. Carritte later testified that he saw a bucket of water standing on the kitchen table suddenly become agitated and begin to boil. A voice was heard in the house talking to Esther and telling her all sorts of horrible things.

Soon after this, a lighted match fell from the ceiling onto the bed. Then eight or ten other lighted matches fell down through the air. Almost all of them started fires, but members of the family were quick to extinguish them. For several days this fire-setting continued. From cellar to attic, the blazes continued to be lighted, and members of the household lived in constant danger of having the house burn down over their heads.

One night Esther shouted that the ghost had appeared to her. "My God," she cried, "don't you see him too? He says I must leave this house tonight or he will kindle a fire in the loft and burn us all to death. Where shall I go?"

In his desperation Daniel Teed thought of his good friend John White and took Esther to White's home. White agreed to let her stay. Then, four weeks after Esther had changed homes, the ghost suddenly reappeared. A clasp knife that belonged to little Frederick White was whisked out of his grasp and embedded in Esther's back. Fred pulled it out, whereupon it was taken from him and inserted in the same wound. Others came to her rescue and took the knife away.

In December, Esther became ill with diphtheria and was confined to her bed for a little over two weeks. During her sickness, the ghost did not try to bother her at all. Recovering from the illness, Esther went to Sackville, New Brunswick, for a visit with her other sister, Mrs. John Snowden, and was free from the ghost in this new location.

Esther then returned to Amherst and occupied a different

room. One night she told her sister Jennie that another ghost had just informed her that the old ghost was coming back to set the house on fire. The next day the members of the family gathered to discuss the message in Esther's room, and a lighted match fell from the ceiling as they talked. Within the next few minutes eight or ten matches fell, but they were all extinguished. That night the loud noises began again.

Now another amazing thing happened. When the noises began, Daniel Teed shouted out to the ghost, asking if it could tell how many were in the room. "Give a knock for each person on the floor," Teed cried. Immediately there were six distinct knocks for the six persons actually present in the room. From that time on, the members of the family could speak to the ghost in this fashion. The ghost would knock once for a negative answer, three times for an affirmative, and twice if it were not sure of the answer.

Daniel asked the ghost if the house would really be set on fire and the ghost answered with two knocks. Five minutes later the invisible ghost grabbed a dress from a nail on the wall, rolled it up under the bed, and set it on fire. Daniel pulled the flaming garment from under the bed before any serious damage had been done and extinguished the blaze.

All the members of the family were now convinced that the ghost was that of some very evil person who had once lived on the earth and who, for some strange reason, had decided to torture poor Esther. One method of extreme torture was to adopt the strange technique of "moving about in her abdomen, which caused her to swell so fearfully and feel like bursting." The ghost also perpetrated another torture on the girl, but during my visits to Amherst I was merely able to learn that it was of such intimate nature that I should not discuss it.

When the ghost threatened to kindle fires in the White residence, John White asked Esther if she would accompany him to his tavern so that he could keep his eyes on the ghost while he was working. Esther consented, and soon the ghost also began to appear at the tavern. One morning the door of the large cooking stove was opened and shut incessantly by the ghost. Finally Mr. White braced it with an axe handle. Suddenly the ghost lifted the door from its hinges, and sent it flying, along with the ax handle, up into the air to crash heavily on the floor several feet away!

Furious with rage and astonishment, Mr. White rushed out of doors and shouted to Mr. W. H. Rogers, inspector of fisheries for Nova Scotia, who happened to be passing by, to come inside and witness this phenomenon. They entered the kitchen, and White rehung the door, bracing it again with the ax handle. At once the door flew off with the ax handle and both landed several feet away!

At another time three large iron spikes were placed on Esther's lap while she was sitting in the dining room of the tavern. The spikes began to turn red hot, and then they flew through the air to the other end of the tavern, twenty feet away. This happened in the presence of a group of local citizens. Among those present from time to time, who came as unbelievers and went away admitting that some supernatural power was operating, were William Hillson, Daniel Morrison, Robert Hutchinson, and the editor of the Amherst *Gazette,* J. Albert Black. All of the men mentioned were well-known citizens of Amherst in 1879.

The Amherst mystery attracted so much attention that Mr. Walter Hubbell, a popular tragedian of the day, became intensely interested in it and decided to debunk the affair as a hoax. Arriving in Amherst on June 11, 1879, the actor visited the home of Esther Cox and met her for the first time. Within a few days Hubbell was definitely convinced that there was something genuine about the whole affair, and the man who arrived to scoff remained to believe. Not only was he certain that the ghost was an actuality, but he made plans to take Esther on a tour and exhibit her.

On June 12 Esther Cox, Mr. White, and Walter Hubbell went to the Amherst railway station to take the train for Moncton, New Brunswick, where Esther was scheduled to appear. A large crowd had gathered and among them was a man who had failed in his attempts to persuade Esther to go on a lecture tour with him. It is believed from what happened later that the man surreptitiously boarded the same train to make trouble for them in Moncton. Arriving in Moncton, the group stopped at the American House, and that same night the ghost began to start a chair rocking fifteen feet away from Esther. The newspapers of the period covered the entire affair very well, and I now quote from the Moncton *Despatch* of June 18, 1879:

Miss Esther Cox arrived here in care of friends, on Friday afternoon last, and a detailed account of the manifestations and working of the mystery were given in Ruddick's Hall, on Friday evening and Saturday. Sunday evening, Miss Cox essayed to attend service at the Baptist Church, but during the first singing, the ghost which had been quiet for some days, again manifested itself by knocking, apparently, on the floor of the pew in front. When told to stop by Miss Cox, it would cease the noise for a moment, but then break out worse than ever. Throughout the prayer it continued; and when the organ began for the second singing, the noise became so distinct and disturbing that Miss Cox and party were forced to leave the church. Upon reaching the house on Wesley Street, where they were stopping, the ghost seemed to enter into Miss Cox, and she was sick and insensible until morning. Lying upon the bed, she seemed for a time in great pain, her chest heaving as though in a rapid succession of hiccoughs, and her body and limbs being very much swollen. A medical gentleman of this town, who saw her at the time, stated that the symptoms were those of a functional heart disease, probably caused by nervous excitement.

The heart was beating at an exceedingly rapid rate, and the lungs seemed gorged with blood, so that a portion was forced into the stomach, causing the patient to vomit blood afterwards. A sound could be distinctly heard in the region of the heart, resembling the shaking of water in a muffled bottle, supposed to be caused by the blood in a cavity being shaken by the violent hiccough motion of the body. As to the cause of the affection, that is a mystery. Toward morning Miss Cox relapsed into a state of somnolence and late in the day awoke, seeming entirely recovered. She states, however, that on Monday afternoon, while sitting near the window of a room on the ground floor, a fan dropped out of the window; she went outside to recover it, and on returning, a chair, from the opposite side of the room, was found upside down near the door, as though it had attempted to follow her out of the room. No one else witnessed this occurrence.

Again, while writing, the ghost took possession of the pen, and wrote in a different hand altogether other and entirely different words from what were intended; in fact, it wrote of itself, the young lady being able to look in another direction, and not to show the least interest in what the pen was writing. A gentleman, who was present at the time, asked the ghost its name, when it wrote in reply, "Maggie Fisher," and stated that she had gone to the red school-house on the hill, in Upper Stewiacke, before Miss Cox did but left when she went. Miss Cox did not know this Maggie Fisher, but it seems that at one time she did attend the school indicated, and that a girl of that name, now dead, had attended previously. Monday night, Miss Cox was again attacked and held under the power of the ghost, much the same as the night previous.

A representative of the *Despatch* called on Esther Cox yesterday afternoon, but, she not being under the power, of course, no manifestations could be seen. The lady appeared quite pleasant and affable, and looked well. She considers her trouble to be a ghost, and is more perplexed with it than any one else. She says she cannot tell, by any premonitory symptoms, when the manifestations are going to commence, is becoming rather frightened concerning it and is very easily annoyed and excited by any noise, except that which she herself may cause. If the ghost is willing, Miss Cox will leave for Chatham, by train today.

The Halifax *Presbyterian Witness* in June 1879 was outspoken on the matter:

The Amherst Mystery, we are informed on the best authority, is no mystery at all, except to persons who refrain from using their powers of observation and reason. The only mystery is that so many persons who should know better are deceived. The newspapers are greatly to blame for "working up" this pitiable sensation. The story is now going the rounds that the girl, Esther Cox, is to be taken around on exhibition. In the name of humanity, propriety, religion, and decency, we earnestly protest against a proceeding so base and disgusting. If the girl is sick, why should her infirmities be exhibited to the public? If, on the other hand there is nothing to exhibit but very clumsy tricks of legerdemain, the exhibitors will at least appear before the public in a *role* not worthy of character.

The group left Moncton on June 18, headed for Chatham, New Brunswick, about eighty miles to the north. It is believed that the man who failed to obtain Miss Cox on his tour was in the audience the night she appeared on the stage of the Chatham theater.

As Mr. Hubbell was delivering the concluding remarks of his speech that evening, he was interrupted when an old man in the audience arose, shook his cane, and shouted, "Young man, beware!"

Hubbell continued with his speech in spite of the interruption and had Esther stand up and bow just as the curtain was rung down. Immediately afterward there was a great amount of loud talking in the pit of the theater, and a moment later Mr. White rushed into the wings to tell Mr. Hubbell that a ruffian had attempted to strike him. Hubbell asked White if he had obtained their share of the receipts, and White told him that he had the money.

Ten minutes later the three reached the street and ran into a howling mob. Hubbell grabbed Esther by the arm and started through the crowd. Brickbats and stones were thrown at them, but no one was hit. Finally they reached their hotel, all three completely unnerved by their experience. Mr. White declared that as far as he was concerned the tour was over, for they would surely all be killed before they ended their long journey around Nova Scotia and New Brunswick.

A short time later a friend of the group reached the hotel, where he told Hubbell that another and greater demonstration was planned for the following day. His advice was for them to leave by the night train for Amherst. Hubbell accepted the advice, and the three went aboard the train at midnight. Thus ended the tour of the Great Amherst Mystery, on June 20, 1879.

A few days later, the ghost really caused trouble. At breakfast the lid of the sugar bowl flew off and finally dropped down from the ceiling. Hubbell himself saw it suspended one foot from the ceiling before it crashed. Entering the parlor, Hubbell saw a large potted plant sail away from the window. It was followed by a tin pail half full of water, which came to rest beside the plant on the middle of the parlor floor. That same day Esther's face was slapped by the ghost.

By now the malignant spirit had been identified as a certain Bob Nickle. There were other ghosts, too, according to Esther: Maggie Fisher, twenty-one years of age, who had been dead twelve years; her sister Mary; Peter Teed; John Nickle; and Eliza MacNeal. But the ringleader was Bob Nickle, and Hubbell describes him as a scheming scoundrel, sixty years of age, who had been a shoemaker when he was on earth.

Hubbell was remarking one day that the gray-and-white family cat had never been harmed when suddenly it was lifted from the floor to a height of five feet and then dropped on Esther's back. That night the ghost of Bob Nickle entered the girls' bedroom and tore their nightgowns. Two days later the ghost again acted in a terrible fashion. He threw knives around the house and moved the loft trap door. The next day he began sticking pins into Esther's body. Hubbell tells us that he spent most of the day pulling pins from Esther.

On Friday, June 27, a trumpet sounded all day long, and Esther told the others that Nickle was blowing it. Mr. Hubbell found the trumpet later and kept it for the rest of his life.

On another occasion Mr. Hubbell desired a light for his pipe, and spoke out, "Bob, I would like a match, if you please." At once a shower of matches fell from the ceiling. Mr. Hubbell declared that he could tell which ghost was in action because of the difference in the knocking. The ghost of Maggie knocked in a soft and delicate fashion, while Bob Nickle knocked with terrible sledgehammer blows.

Walter Hubbell believed that the true story behind the mystery lay in a terrible experience of Esther's on August 28, 1878. She had gone buggy riding with Bob MacNeal, a young friend. Reaching a secluded part of Amherst, Bob attempted to force her out of the carriage to walk in the forest. He pulled out a revolver, aimed the gun at her heart, and demanded that she come into the woods with him or he would kill her. She refused his demands. He repeated them, again pointing the revolver at her heart, swearing terribly all the while. Cocking the gun, he was apparently about to fire when the sound of an approaching carriage made him change his mind.

Leaping into the buggy where Esther was still seated, Bob seized the reins and drove home at a furious clip. On the drive back into Amherst it rained heavily, and when they reached the Princess Street cottage, Esther's clothing was wet through to her body. She was in a serious, hysterical condition because of her experience. Later, when Hubbell investigated the boy's background, he found that among other strange habits, Bob MacNeal had been fond of skinning cats alive and releasing them to run around the neighborhood until they died.

Hubbell felt that the attempt of Bob MacNeal to force Esther out of the carriage and commit an outrage upon her affected her mind and caused a derangement of her entire system. While deranged, he reasoned, her vital magnetism escaped, and thus she became a person subject to the power of the ghosts of the dead. Hubbell also believed that Bob MacNeal was obsessed by the evil spirit of Bob Nickle, the old shoemaker. Upon reaching the grove, the evil spirit of the older man completely dominated the youth, according to

Hubbell's reasoning. Thus the older man, really acting out the one desire of his devilish nature through the organism of Bob MacNeal, forced the boy to act as he did. Shortly after the incident Bob MacNeal left Amherst for good. An interesting aftermath of the affair was a discovery that both Bob Nickle and Bob MacNeal were shoemakers.

Years later, the demons were chased away from Esther by the "incantations and conjurations of an 'Indian Medicine Man' or 'Witch Doctor' " and they promised never to follow or molest her again." The ghost then visited Bob MacNeal and bothered him for several years afterward.

Another remarkable thing about the mystery should be noted. The ghostly manifestations began on September 4, 1878, and always returned with the greatest strength about every twenty-eight days afterward. The changes of the moon were given as the reason for this twenty-eight-day cycle, but other investigators had thought that the ghost cycle had more to do with the girl herself.

After leaving her home at the insistence of the landlord, who did not wish his house to burn down, Esther Cox obtained a position working for Mr. Arthur Davison. One day, when Esther was present, Davison's barn burned down, and he had her arrested for starting the fire. The judge and jury did not believe in ghosts and Esther was sentenced to four months in jail. After being in prison for one month, she was released because of public sentiment in her favor.

Many years later, in 1893, Arthur Davison wrote a statement regarding the entire incident from which I quote:

I do not believe in Spiritualism. My own idea is that in some way the magnetic power in this girl became unhinged. . . . Esther Cox worked for me for three months and a better one we never had since we have been married, (20 years). I have often watched her to find out how she came down stairs, she seemed to fly. It proved a bad day for me before she left, as she burned my barn. I may say in passing I read the book published by Hubbell, and while he painted the facts up to make the book sell, the facts were there all the same. She was not good looking, very ignorant, only a common education, could read and write but not spell. She was very much afraid of it. I tried several times to teach her to exert control of her will power, but just as I had gained a point she became afraid and would go no farther nor do anything. My house and where she lived before she came to live with me was only about fifty yards distant and I used to call often to see how she got along. Hundreds did the same.

At first it was only rapping and pounding, but at times it assumed a more serious aspect. One night as I was on my way home, I met the Doctor who attended her. . . . He asked me to go with him and see Esther, as he feared she was going to die. He had then tried everything to arouse her from a semi-unconscious state and as a last resort was going to try a battery. When I saw her she was on a cot bed, and seemed to be dead, but for a violent heaving of her body, that is from her breast down to her legs, she would fill up and lift the clothes as you inflate a bladder and then it would suddenly collapse. . . . She had several of these turns but this one I saw; but it is hard to describe it fully but it was the hardest scene I ever witnessed. . . .

Another: And this was the only thing that gave me any fright; I kept a horse and a cow at the time. Esther used to milk the cow. I attended the horse myself. The cow stood at the further end of the barn (say 25 feet from the door) where I kept a box with my curry comb and brushes. This particular evening she had just finished milking and met me at the door. As I stepped inside I saw my curry comb running along the floor about eight or ten feet behind her. You may depend that I stepped out of the way quick too. It struck the door post. I then picked it up, and after that I kept the key in my pocket. The next evening when I came home she wanted the key to go and milk. I handed it to her, she had the milk bucket in her other hand, and just as our hands met, a large 2 quart dipper of water, which had been on the table struck our hands and spilled the water over the both of us, giving me a pretty good wetting, spoiling my cuffs. It appears she had just been using this dipper but it was sitting six or eight feet from us and had to pass through an open door at right angles to get where it did.

My wife saw ashes, tea leaves, scrubbing brushes, soap and mop rags and an old ham bone often flying around and sometimes it put them out in their work, but we got so used to it we put up with all these things as it was hard at the time to get help, especially help like her, until she set my barn on fire, we then had her put in jail, since then I don't know if she has had any of her turns. . . .[Signed] ARTHUR DAVISON, Clerk of County Court, Amherst, Nova Scotia.

After her experiences with the ghost, Esther Cox married —first, a Mr. Adams in Springdale, Nova Scotia, and, when he died, a man named Shanahan. She lived in Brockton, Massachusetts, many years before her death in 1912.

In 1908, twenty-nine years after he had first visited Esther Cox and had taken her on the tour, Walter Hubbell returned to Amherst, Nova Scotia. There he found that the house was still standing, and rented a room in it, where he wrote an addition to his book, calling it *Thirty Years After.* Before he left Amherst he was presented with a testimonial document signed by sixteen well-known citizens of that town. I quote excerpts from that testimonial:

We, the undersigned inhabitants of the Town of Amherst, County of Cumberland, Providence of Nova Scotia . . . having of our own personal knowledge and not by or through hearsay or belief, absolutely known, seen, and heard individually all or some of the demonstrations, manifestations, and communications of an invisible, intelligent and malicious power within the atmosphere that continued its awe-inspiring and mysterious operations in the home of Daniel Teed, 6 Princess Street, Amherst, Nova Scotia, and elsewhere in the actual presence of his sister-in-law Esther Cox (but never manifested itself during her absence from the house) and continued to manifest itself for the period of one year from 1878 to 1879, as narrated by Walter Hubbell the actor . . . which account having been read by us and being known to us as accurate and truthful as to all and each fact . . . we hereto, of our own free will, affix our names to this testamentary paper so that it may . . . go before the world in corroboration and verification of what actually transpired in the presence of the Teeds, Walter Hubbell, and hundreds of the inhabitants of Amherst, including myselves, some thirty years ago.

Signed by us and delivered to Walter Hubbell whom we each know personally, this tenth day of June A.D., 1908.

[Signed]

Daniel Teed	William Ripley
Olive Teed	David T. Chapman
Neander Quigley	John W. Stewart
J. A. Simpson	Lawrence White

Arthur W. Moffatt
J. Albert Black
Silas A. McNutt
William Beattie

Rufus Hicks
Charles Tupper Hillson
Ephraim T. Chapman
Barry D. Bent

In all, I spent several days visiting men of Amherst who could recall the great mystery. All agreed that it was not a hoax and that something spiritual and uncanny had occurred there. Frederick L. Blair, who examined the ruins of the Teed house with me, said, "I know the Amherst mystery to be true. There is not the slightest doubt about it. I have heard the rappings in the house and knew that they were coming from there. It was spiritualism—that is the only way it can be explained."

5

Cotton Mather and
the Invisible World

A study of the overwhelmingly portentous subject of witches, with particular emphasis on New England and Massachusetts, may help you decide what to believe and what not to believe concerning this mental epidemic of several hundred years ago. What I attempt to do in this chapter is to give you the story of the witch horror, and indeed it was a horror, which descended on Massachusetts late in the seventeenth century.

The history of that peculiar mental malady known as witchcraft is awesomely interesting. New England witchcraft is merely the outgrowth of a real, terrible delusion in the Old World which did not stop until thousands and thousands of innocent victims had been executed. That people should be accused of joining with Satan to overcome the powers of righteousness is hard to understand, but why those accused in many cases so readily admitted their guilt is indeed a mystery. Of course, weak minds are often so affected that their owners become unbalanced when faced with an overwhelming crisis, and when we realize that delusions and deceptions can spread with the speed of a forest fire, this is more than unfortunate.

Although Salem is famous the world over as the scene of the witchcraft delusion of 1692, I hasten to tell my readers that executions for witchcraft and charges that one had "communed with the Devil" go back to the earliest days of history. Nevertheless, when the violence began, the Salem witchcraft outbreak was regarded by many as a deep plot to destroy the protestant church in New England and establish the kingdom of Satan. Actually, there were many who believed that the devil himself was personally running the campaign for evil to triumph over good.

Without question, the outbreak was religious fanaticism and sheer ignorance, always strong incentives to action, but it did not all begin in Salem by any means. On September 28, 1652, John Bradstreet of Rowley was convicted in Ipswich Court for having "familiarity with the Devil," while six years later John Godfrey of Andover was accused of causing several people to have "some affliction in their bodies."

In November 1669, Goody Burt was brought to trial because of having wrought effects which were so unusual that they could be attributed to "no natural causes." Her misdeeds took place in Lynn, Marblehead, and Salem. In 1679 Caleb Powell was arrested for "suspicion of working with the Devil to the molesting of William Morse and his family."

Robert Calef, an obscure Boston clothier, proved himself a champion of wisdom when he decided to strike out against this awesome superstition which had been gnawing at the vitals of New England religious life. We of today praise Calef for his courage and tenacity of spirit in the face of overwhelming opposition. Not only do I believe that we should applaud his action, but I also offer the thought that Calef should be included among the spiritual benefactors of his age.

It is hard for us to realize just what was taking place in New England during this period. Although it was the duty of the clergy of Massachusetts to stamp out attacks on the doctrines of the church and to advise on other matters, many spiritual leaders failed completely in their efforts to handle the witchcraft problem with sagacity. The ministers, as men "deeply learned in such things," were appealed to by magistrates and judges for guidance and help. Feebly responding to the appeal, the men of God put on their armor of righteousness and ordered days of fasting and prayer, which they thought the most suitable method for challenging the terrible emergency. Unfortunately, they did little else of a constructive nature. The fact is that, in spite of the certain knowledge that witch hunts and scares on the European continent had been responsible for the deaths by torture of more than 30,000 persons, the members of the clergy in Massachusetts failed to realize that the same frenzy could strike in America.

The major New England trouble began during the winter of 1691–92 in the home of a Salem preacher, the Reverend Mr. Samuel Parris, when a Barbados slave named Tituba became extremely friendly with two children in the family, Abigail and Elizabeth Parris. Working in the household, Tituba actually hypnotized the two girls, who soon accused several people in the community of being witches. To make matters worse, the two girls were taken seriously by the older and presumably more intelligent residents of Salem.

The witch scare spread in leaps and bounds, resulting in those people who were accused being tried in court and sentenced to death. On June 10, 1692, occurred the first hanging of a so-called witch, that of the unfortunate Bridget Bishop, which was followed by the eventual execution of no fewer than twenty people that same year!

Luckily, the new leader of Massachusetts, Governor William Phips,* arrived in New England and took steps which put an end to "all such foolishness," and matters gradually drifted back to a more normal approach to life.**

As was eventually proved in New England, the delusions of the late seventeenth century can be blamed on the mental condition of those who believed in them. Then, as in generations before in Europe, the disease spread like wildfire. Is it possible, at this late date, to blame even one of the New England incidents on anything but deluded minds guided by immature beliefs? Are we really to believe, as spokesmen of the period then claimed, that the devil was making a determined effort to root out the Christian religion in New England?

Samuel Adams Drake tells us that the ministers "took a prominent part," in attempting to entrap the supposed witches, visiting them in jail and asking them leading questions. In this way, we are told, they put into practice the principle that

> The godly may allege
> For anything their privilege,

---

*Phips had been in the West Indies, where he had found $1 million in gold under the sea.

**Whenever visitors to Salem arrive, they ask to see where the witches were burned there. Of course, this is impossible, for no witches ever were burned in Salem. Cambridge and Roxbury were the scenes of such occurrences.

A man witch is still called a warlock. Distinctions also were made between witches, conjurers, and sorcerers. Witches bargained with evil spirits so that they could get their own way, but conjurers, by force of magical words, tried to compel the devil to carry out their wishes. Sorcerers are said to have produced effects beyond the ordinary by words or images.

And to the Devil himself may go,
If they have motives thereunto;
For as there is a war between
The Dev'l and them, it is no sin
If they, by subtle stratagem,
Make use of him as he does them.

Cotton Mather was the foremost clergyman of those dark days. Nevertheless, no fair-minded student of witchcraft would deny that he aided and abetted the growth of the witchcraft scare. He directed all his abilities and learning to get rid of the "devils." As Mather tells us in his *Wonders of the Invisible World,* these demons were walking about the streets "with lengthened chains," creating a dreadful noise. "Brimstone," he explained, "was making a horrid and hellish stench" in men's nostrils.

Brilliant and persuasive, Mather had a personal magnetism or charisma that gave him a large following. Unfortunately, he now threw his weight with all its force to strengthen the delusion, thereby aggravating its disastrous consequences. Although he pretended to be sincere, I have found it easy to doubt him as I study the events of the last few weeks of the delusion. He was simply too fond of the spotlight.

John Greenleaf Whittier wrote in full accord with my present viewpoint. Drake agrees, but adds that the same thoughts concerning Mather with equal fairness might include almost all the Christian ministers of Mather's time.

Robert Calef had the nerve and determination to confront the great Cotton Mather, a preacher who held ancient and modern lore at his tongue's end and was gifted with "fluency, vivacity, and readiness" in composing and writing that might make an even bolder antagonist hesitate to attack him. Calef, a simple, ordinary clothier, unknown outside of the relatively obscure neighborhood where he lived, became a David who spoke out and faced his own Goliath.

The controversy began in 1698 when Calef wrote to Dr. Mather and questioned not only the witchcraft proceedings but the delusion itself. Mather, in his diary on May 10, 1698, calls Calef "a man who makes little conscience of lying."

A young woman of Mather's own congregation, Margaret Rule, whose unusual afflictions had just been published by Mather under the startling caption of *Another Brand pluckt from the Burning,* was said to have been haunted by no less than eight malignant spectres. She had been led on by a demon who, when she refused to join with the devil, tortured her repeatedly. He pinched her, scorched her, stuck pins in her flesh, and on once occasion forced her into convulsions, after which he lifted her bodily from the bed on which she lay. People who visited her would often be choked with the fumes of brimstone rising in the bedchamber, according to Mather.

Taking alarm, Robert Calef dreaded a new outbreak of the witch delusion, whose embers then "were still smouldering." He began to distrust both the integrity and the wisdom of Cotton Mather and announced that he openly opposed Mather in the field of religion and public policy. Calef carried out his opposition with surprising ability and vigor and showed that he had a well-equipped arsenal of scriptural learning at his command.

In sneering fashion, Cotton Mather reacted to Calef's opposition, referring to Calef as the "weaver turned minister." Calef retaliated by becoming more definite in his accusations, and the clothier who at first was despised became a man whose reason was never "overthrown by panic." Mather, confident of his ability to subdue Calef, greatly underestimated his antagonist.

After Mather's story of Margaret Rule had been made public, Calef drew up and circulated his own thoughts on the subject, based on the statements of other eyewitnesses. His efforts became a definite protest against the methods used by Mather to draw out extravagant, incoherent statements from the afflicted girl.

Calef's action caused Mather to be greatly offended, and the preacher "retorted with abusive epithets" and threatened Calef with an action for slander. Calef was arrested on a warrant for uttering "scandalous libels" and was bound over in court, but the case never did come to trial.

Calef kept at his task to prevent a return to the witchcraft horrors of 1692, which he called the "sorest affliction and greatest blemish to religion" that ever struck the new world of Englishmen in America.

A strong reaction to the witch hunt now set in all over New England, and those who had been the most forward in abetting the witchcraft proceedings began to plan a way to openly admit their mistakes.

On January 14, 1697, witch judge Samuel Sewall stood up in the congregation and handed the usher a statement to be read by the pastor. He remained standing until the minister read aloud Sewall's admission of the error of his ways. This memorable confession was never forgotten by those who heard it, and there is a belief that on every January 14 for the remainder of his life, Sewall carried out a private service of prayer and humility.

Encouraged by Sewall's public confession and the admission of others of their erroneous parts in the witch crisis, Calef continued to press Cotton Mather rigorously.

Mather, however, did attempt to explain himself in his story of Margaret Rule. "Why," he asks, "after all my un- wearied cares and pains to rescue the miserable from the lions and bears of hell, which had seized them . . . must I be driven to the necessity of an apology?" Indeed, Cotton Mather hated to apologize for his previous stand, for it was hard for him to descend "from his high pedestal." Mather could not endure ridicule. He said that "some of our learned witlings of the coffee house, for fear lest these proofs of an Invisible World should spoil some of their sport, will endeavor to turn them all into sport."

However, the witchcraft delusion, as Samuel Adams Drake wrote, had reached the end of its "blood-corroded chain." Nevertheless, the sickening thought persisted that the judges who had decreed the deaths of many innocent persons had effectively stopped men's tongues from speaking, unless, as did Calef, they spoke out from the necessity of conscience.

Actually, attempting to understand the witch delusion is like working on a jigsaw puzzle with only half of the pieces available.

In 1700 Robert Calef printed in London, after he had been refused permission for publication in this country, the facts in his controversy with Cotton Mather. He added an "Impartial Account" of the Salem witch outbreak and a review of Mather's life of Sir William Phips. Calef called the volume *More Wonders of an Invisible World*. When the volume arrived in Boston it was hurriedly taken to Harvard Yard in Cambridge, where it was publicly burned by order of the president of Harvard.

Poet Whittier refers to this in his verses entitled "Calef in Boston." The fourth stanza, which I quote below refers to the Margaret Rule incident. Mather had related how the demons who tortured the girl had puppets into which they would thrust pins whenever they wished to hurt her.

As many of my readers know, this followed an ancient superstition. It is said that witches often would make images in wax of persons against whom they held a grudge. By sticking pins into the images, they actually tortured their victims in the flesh, it was believed. As early as 1100 B.C. several women in the harem of Ramses III made wax images of their pharaoh.

We are told that Socrates said "There is only one good, namely knowledge, and only one evil, ignorance." How this great man of Greece would explain the witchcraft evil is hard to say. In any case, do not forget what Thomas Hardy wrote centuries later: "Though there is a good deal too strange to be believed, nothing is too strange to have happened."

Having expressed our thoughts on witchcraft, let us quote Whittier, the bard of Amesbury:

CALEF IN BOSTON
John Greenleaf Whittier

In the solemn days of old
  Two men met in Boston town,
One a tradesman frank and bold,
  One a preacher of renown.

Cried the last, in bitter tone:
  "Poisoner of the wells of truth!
Satan's hireling, thou hast sown
  With his tares the heart of youth!"

Spake the simple tradesman then:
  "God be judge 'twixt thou and I;
All thou knowest of truth hath been
  Unto men like thee a lie.

.　.　.

"Of your spectral puppet play
  I have traced the cunning wires;
Come what will, I needs must say,
  God is true, and ye are liars."

When the thought of man is free,
  Error fears its lightest tones;
So the priest cried, "Sadducee!"
  And the people took up stones.

In the ancient burying-ground,
  Side by side, the twain now lie,—
One with humble grassy mound,
  One with marbles pale and high.

6

Phantom Ships

Or of that Phantom Ship, whose form
Shoots like a meteor through the storm;
When the dark scud comes driving hard,
And lowered is every topsail yard,
And canvas, wove in earthly looms,
No more to brave the storm presumes!
Then, mid the war of sea and sky,
Top and topgallant hoisted high
Full spread and crowded every sail,
The Demon Frigate braves the gale;
And well the doom'd spectators know
The harbinger of wreck and woe.

So wrote Sir Walter Scott more than a century and a half
ago. This brilliant writer and poet offers all of us a chance
in the poem above to fall under the spell of his genius.

At the height of an unbelievably furious gale, a Dutch

captain was sailing off the tip end of South Africa, attempting to round the Cape of Good Hope against a head wind. Just what did happen before he finished his doubling of that famous cape will probably never be agreed upon, but as a result of this voyage, according to some, the captain from Holland became known as the Flying Dutchman.

More than a quarter century ago J. G. Lockhart told us that there is often no clear border between the mystery and the myth, and especially does this apply to the Flying Dutchman. If we can strip the legend of the wrappings in which generations of superstitions have enveloped it, perhaps we can accept the original story.

If it did take place, the voyage occurred hundreds of years ago. But even within the last hundred years the story of the Dutchman was firmly believed by many mariners, and it is only with the advent of the fast steamers and the trans-Atlantic passenger airplanes that it has lost some of its vitality. Although formerly the Flying Dutchmen was a real being to thousands of sailors, he has now become so exclusively a myth that the extent to which his story might have been true tends to be ignored today.

Many writers have contributed to make the tale an everlasting one. Whittier employed the Flying Dutchman as background in his "The Dead Ship of Harpswell," Wagner used the theme of Vanderdecken in *Der Fliegende Hollander,* while Coleridge in his *Ancient Mariner* and Marryat in *The Phantom Ship* both drew on the legendary story.

Three great authorities, Rokeby, Bechstein, and Thorpe, agree essentially that the Flying Dutchman was a nobleman in the thirteenth century who murdered his bride and his brother in a fit of passion when he believed that he had discovered them together in an embarrassing situation on his wedding night, but it was later found that he had been wrong.

Condemned forever to wander toward the north, he arrived at the seashore near Haarlem. There he found a man awaiting him with a boat. As he entered the boat, the man said, "Expectamus te." Then, according to the legend, the captain, attended by his good and evil spirit, rowed toward a spectral bark in the harbor, boarded her, and assumed command. Soon they were sailing out of the bay with all sails set. He has been sailing ever since that time, almost seven centuries, while his good and evil spirits play dice for his soul.

Should you encounter him and his craft in the North Sea, according to Fletcher Bassett, it will be easy to identify his craft and his crew. Without helmsman or helm, the Flying Dutchman always is sailing northward. The ship is painted gray, has varicolored sails, a pale flag, and no crew of any kind!

Frankly, there is no reason why the legend of the Flying Dutchman could not have had a historical origin. Possibly he was a Dutchman named Bernard Fokke who lived centuries ago. A reckless seaman, Fokke encased his masts with iron so that he could carry more sail in storms. It was always understood that he had made a pact with the devil, which explained his marvelous feats at sea. For example, he sailed to the East Indies in ninety days! Finally he disappeared, and it was believed that Satan had at last taken him. People say that his spectral ship may be seen off the Cape of Good Hope, manned by Fokke and three sailors. When he hails passing vessels, the sailor is warned to ignore him for the good of his soul and the safety of his body. Fletcher S. Bassett, in *Legends and Superstitions of the Sea,* tells us that sometimes a boat will be seen approaching the phantom ship and that on reaching it the boat will disappear. A short time later the ship will vanish too.

There is another story regarding the Flying Dutchman involving a Dutch captain who feared neither God nor saints. All went well until he came near the Cape of Good Hope, where he ran into head winds strong enough to "blow the horns off a bull." All the passengers prayed for the captain to turn back, but he refused. His masts came tumbling down and his sails were carried away, but he laughed and smoked his pipe. When the crew attempted to force him to make for the shelter of a bay nearby, he grabbed the ringleader and flung him overboard to his death in the sea. Even as he did so the clouds above opened up and a form alighted on the quarterdeck.

This form is said to have been the Almighty himself, but the Captain went on smoking his pipe and did not even touch his cap when the form addressed him. Let us have Auguste Jal in his *Scènes de la Vie Maritime* finish the story:

"Captain," said the Form, "you are very stubborn."

"And you are a rascal," cried the Captain. "Who wants a peaceful passage? I don't. I'm asking nothing from you, so clear out of this if you don't want your brains blown out."

The Form gave no other answer than a shrug of the shoulders. The Captain then snatched up a pistol, cocked it, and fired; but the bullet, instead of reaching its target, pierced his own hand. His fury knew no bounds. He leaped up to strike the Form in the face with his fist, but his arm dropped limply to his side as though paralyzed. In his impotent rage he cursed and blasphemed and called the good God all sorts of impious names.

But the Form said to him: "Henceforth you are accursed, condemned to sail on forever without rest or anchorage or port of any kind. You shall have neither beer nor tobacco. Gall shall be your drink and red-hot iron your meat. Of your crew your cabin-boy alone shall remain with you; horns shall grow out of his forehead, and he shall have the muzzle of a tiger and skin rougher than that of a dogfish."

The Captain groaned, but the Form continued: "It shall ever be your watch, and when you wish, you will not be able to sleep, for directly you close your eyes a sword shall pierce your body. And since it is your delight to torment sailors, you shall torment them."

The Captain smiled.

"For you shall be the evil spirit of the sea. You shall traverse all latitudes without respite or repose, and your ship shall bring misfortune to all who sight it."

"Amen to that!" cried the Captain with a shout of laughter.

"And on the Day of Judgment Satan shall claim you."

"A fig for Satan!" was all the Captain answered.

The Almighty disappeared, and the Dutchman found himself alone with his cabin-boy, who was already changed as had been predicted. The rest of his crew had vanished.

From that day forward the Flying Dutchman has sailed the seas, and it is his pleasure to plague poor mariners. He casts away their ship on an uncharted shoal, sets them on a false course, and then shipwrecks them. He turns their wine sour and all their food into beans. Sometimes he will send letters on board the ships he meets, and if the Captain tries to read them, he is lost, or an empty boat will draw alongside the Phantom Ship and disappear, a sure sign of ill-fortune. He can change at will the appearance of his ship, so as not to be recognized; and round him he has collected a crew as cursed as himself, all the criminals, pirates, and cowards of the sea.

How much of the above is true? Probably there was such a captain and without question there have been many sightings of such a craft, but where should we draw the line between fact and myth?

The average illiterate sailor had no way of committing his legends to paper, and of course there is no way of proving that the tale is a true one. Nevertheless, I offer that there may have been a Dutchman of evil repute who perished, as many better men have perished since, in trying to round Cape of Good Hope. We may also assume that without question someone came home from sea with news of a strange ship, apparently unmanned, sighted one moment and lost the next. The two events, dissolved into one by the passing of time, became a good story. Such an account would lose little in the telling; it might well begin as a perfectly natural narrative and, improving with each retelling, end with all the delightfully weird circumstances recorded by several authors.

The supernatural always must be reckoned with at sea, for the ocean often plays amazing tricks on many of those who live on the billowy deeps. Otherwise, how can we explain the *Barracouta* affair?

The brig *Barracouta* was one of a squadron in 1821 which was sent to explore the coasts of Arabia, Africa, and Madagascar. In the course of the voyage the squadron separated. Captain Owen, who was on H.M.S. *Severn*, records the following episode:

In the evening of the 6th of April, when off Point Danger, the *Barracouta* was seen about two miles to leeward. Struck with the singularity of her being so soon after us, we at first concluded that it could not be she; but the peculiarity of her rigging and other circumstances convinced us that we were not mistaken. Nay, so distinctly was she seen that many well-known faces could be observed on deck, looking towards our ship.

After keeping thus for some time, we became surprised that she made no effort to join us, but on the contrary stood away. But being so near to the port to which we were both destined, Captain Owen did not attach much importance to this proceeding, and we accordingly continued our course. At sunset it was observed that she hove to and sent a boat away, apparently for the purpose of picking up a man overboard. During the night we could not perceive any light or other indication of her locality. The next morning we anchored in Simon's Bay, where for a whole week we were in anxious expectation of her arrival; but it afterwards appeared that at this very period the *Barracouta* must have been about 300 miles from us, and no other vessel of the same class was ever seen about the Cape.

Before his death in 1960, J. G. Lockhart became fascinated with the story of the *Barracouta* and commented as follows in his *Mysteries of the Sea:*

What was it? The Flying Dutchman? The locality is just right; so is the cunning with which the strange ship assumed the form of the *Barracouta;* so is the boat which was seen putting out from her side. If we could only add that shortly after this apparition the *Severn* met with some terrible disaster, we could scarcely fail to be convinced. But fortunately (or unfortunately for our theory), Captain Owen brought his ship home without mishap. Must we then fall back on science and talk of refraction, or some similar atmospheric freak that might reproduce so startling a mirage?

It is at least possible that some such phenomenon gave rise to the belief that the old Dutch Captain was still afloat; and since it may have been years since he was last spoken of and the mirage may have faded as swiftly and mysteriously as it had appeared, the witnesses might be expected to seek a supernatural explanation of what they had seen.

Most of us who follow the sea in one fashion or another have been impressed by tales of the Flying Dutchman. The name has appeared on many craft down through the years, but the extreme clipper ship *Flying Dutchman,* launched in 1852, is perhaps the most outstanding of all. She was at first very fast, but the hoodoo accompanying the name, said by some to influence her, began in the year 1854, when even fair-minded Matthew Maury spoke of her slowness in reaching the equator.

She left on what was destined to be her last voyage from New York on May 30, 1857. There are tales of mystical beings aboard who influenced the men at the wheel, but she reached San Francisco safely after unfortunate delays around Cape Horn and started back toward New York on November 1, 1857.

Finally she was making good time, being spoken by the *Starlight* forty-two days out and off South America in the Atlantic. Approaching her destination, she suddenly piled up on Brigantine Beach, New Jersey, and proved a total loss. Her name had finally caught up with her.

We should realize that although the average sailor was illiterate, when he returned from his voyage he was bound to talk. He would discuss his adventures in the taverns and inns and speak of the "good old days" with his fellow wanderers.

In November 1949 I talked with South African newsman Errol Friedmann, who had served on Union-Castle Line vessels. At that time he had talked with a number of seamen who swore that they had seen the Flying Dutchman. The sightings were always at night and a strange blue light was always present. The latitudes were between the island of St. Helena and the Cape of Good Hope.

An elderly boatswain stated that he had been a deckhand on the *Dunvegan Castle* in 1940 and saw the Flying Dutchman appear during what was then called "jolly old blackout time." Although not superstitious, the man decided to leave the ship on her return to Southampton and did so, and the craft was torpedoed within a few days of sailing back to South Africa.

7

Were They from Outer Space?

Only a small percentage of the hundreds upon hundreds of sightings of unidentified flying objects—or UFOs as they are often called—can possibly be accepted as reasonable reports. Probably out of one thousand accounts, one of those actually should be considered. Nevertheless, if even this one sighting be accurate, it is more than worthy of consideration. I shall mention several.

Incidentally, the first picture ever made of a flying saucer, it is said, was taken on August 12, 1883. A Professor Bonilla at the Zacatecas Observatory in Mexico was the photographer.

On November 28, 1954, a Venezuelan named Gustavo Gonzales drove his truck from Caracas on the road to Petare a short distance away. His helper, José Ponce, was with him. It was morning and the truck had covered roughly a third of the way when they came to a bend in the road. There they encountered a large round object suspended in the air about five feet above the road, possibly similar to a modern hovercraft.

Frightened but fascinated at what they saw, both men stepped out of the truck. A small person ran toward them. He wore an unusual costume consisting of a light brown loin cloth, and his dark skin was covered with short bristly hair. Suddenly the little man picked up the burly Gonzales and threw him about fifteen feet.

When Ponce saw what had happened, he began running toward the police station which was only a short distance away.

Gonzales then noticed two more of the tiny men approaching the hovercraft, carrying what appeared to be plants which they had pulled up by the roots. Covered with blood from his encounter with the strange little man, Gonzales observed that the creature was approaching him again. Frightened, Gonzales drew his knife and attempted to stab the visitor, but the knife glanced off his opponent's shoulder as though the man himself were made of metal. At this moment something struck Gonzales a glancing blow. Pulling away, he started for the police station.

After being interviewed, Gonzales and Ponce were given a sobriety test which they passed. Sedatives were then administered and the two men fell asleep. Later, when they had had a chance to recover, they repeated their earlier stories in sworn statements.

Surprisingly enough a doctor from the area who had been returning to his home after an emergency call had witnessed the encounter, but he remained silent because, logically enough, he was afraid that his standing in the community would suffer if he reported what he had seen.

Later the doctor did tell everything, giving essentially the same facts that the two men had related. As far as is known, his name was never revealed by the police, who promised not to publicize the doctor's story but used it to substantiate the account of the two men, Gonzales and Ponce.

Another example had taken place seven years before. On August 14, 1947, Professor R. L. Johannis of Carnia, Italy, was walking near his residence when he came across a huge disc more than ten meters wide (32.8 feet), having a cupola and a telescopic metallic antenna.

Seeing two tiny men, Professor Johannis waved his geologist's pick at them, whereupon one of the creatures touched his own belt and Johannis' pick bounced out of his hand as he experienced what apparently was an electric shock.

A few moments later the disclike object rose from the earth, remained stationary for a short time, and then vanished rapidly into the distance. Johannis did not see them again.

The third tale takes the reader back to 1909. I first read of this incident in a book by Charles Fort, who himself was a remarkable man. Always interested in any strange, unbelievable occurrence, he carefully recorded it.*

Fort, who died in 1932, tells the story of Mr. C. Lithbridge who was a dock worker in the winter and a Punch and Judy showman in the summer. On May 16, 1909, Lithbridge, pulling a small cart behind him, was walking home over Caerphilly Mountain near Cardiff, Wales. On reaching the summit, he noticed two small men working near a gigantic tube. Wearing heavy fur overcoats and heavy fur caps pulled closely over their heads, the beings frightened Lithbridge, but he continued to walk toward the people until he was only twenty yards away.

When the men heard the approach of the Lithbridge cart, they jumped up and began to talk in a strange language. Quickly they crawled under the tube and into a carriage which was suspended below.

*His account of a snowflake weighing several hundred pounds which landed in India has always fascinated me.

The strange tubelike craft now rose into the air, zigzagging as it proceeded through the atmosphere in the general direction of Cardiff. As the giant tube left the ground, Lithbridge noticed two great searchlight beams throwing out a strong light. He also was able to identify two wheels under the carriage. As the tube left the area, Lithbridge detected a fan whirling from the tail in a manner probably similar to that of a helicopter of today.

Flying saucers in Massachusetts are few and far between, but on October 17, 1973, one did appear over Route 2 in Acton. Kevin Lawler and his sister Ann Mary Lawler saw it as they were returning from Boston where they had attended their grandmother's funeral. Later I talked with their mother, Jane Lawler, the wife of William Lawler of Fitchburg, Massachusetts.

"My mother had passed away," began Mrs. Lawler, "and we were coming back to Fitchburg after the services in Boston. We were in one car and daughter Ann Mary and son Kevin in their car, which was an Opel GT. We had left some time before them and did not participate or see anything which affected them.

"They were driving on Route 2 in Acton, just where you have to stop at the traffic lights, when suddenly they saw a very brilliant light some distance away in the sky. As they left the stop lights and drove toward the west, they noticed the intense, piercing light getting even brighter.

"It wasn't really dark, and there were no stars out. Just about dusk, I would say. The brilliant light was almost exactly over Route 2. As they drove toward the light, of course, it became brighter and brighter until finally it was hovering right over them. They pulled off the road hoping that some other car would come along and that they could share their overwhelming experience.

"As they described it to me later, they could identify the

oval disc shape of the flying saucer and the fact that the body resembled a sieve. Then they lost their nerve and drove back onto the road and continued westward. Looking back, they noticed that the flying saucer had gained altitude. It soon disappeared into the sky.

"They were asked if it couldn't have been a helicopter, but they were insistent that it couldn't have been.

"Reaching home some time after we did, they were terribly excited when they began to tell my husband and me about their experience. Kevin never gets excited, and there he was just as tense as his sister.

"I said to them, 'All right, settle down and tell us just what did take place.' And they told me the story. Ann Mary, twenty years old, is a student at Fitchburg State College. Kevin goes to Notre Dame High in Fitchburg and is sixteen. Ann called her friend and it became known throughout the country."

Down through the centuries of recorded history, we of the planet Earth have from time to time adopted a variety of classifications involving mysterious beings which may or may not exist on our planet or in the outer universe. Each of us has his own list of doubtful subjects. Some of us choose witches, mermaids, or sea monsters. Others emphasize spectral beings, ghosts, and werewolves. Still others are attracted to the possibility of unidentified flying objects, which allegedly have been seen in various parts of this and other countries.

Scientists are working hard to solve these many mysteries, and almost every man of learning with whom I have talked recently is certain that a breakthrough with beings unknown in other worlds will eventually come.

For those of you who believe that very little progress along these lines is possible, I have only one fair question. Would your great-grandfathers and great-grandmothers of even three-quarters of a century ago have believed that we could send men into space? Or in another comparison, what would our grandfathers and grandmothers of the 1890s think of our being able to pick up a telephone and reserve a place on a jumbo jet which would in a short time take off from our nearest airport with 350 other people and fly hundreds of miles in a few hours at the speed of sound while we watch movies and eat our regular meals.

There are millions of normal people in this country, all deep thinkers, who believe that no other creatures or beings exist in the universe except those in our own important world. Nevertheless, it is my opinion that there is a strong *possibility* that the human race as we know it today is not the only example of life in existence. In the next few pages I hope to convince a few of those millions that they should be open-minded on the subject.

The outstanding men of all walks of life who agree with this possibility are legion, and I draw attention to several of them at this time.

The famed astronomer Dr. Harlow Shapley told me a quarter of a century ago that there were other worlds with "thinking beings" living in them. Dr. Harold C. Urey, known everywhere for his nuclear research, said that it was "exceedingly probable that there is life in the universe more intelligent than ours."

Senator Barry Goldwater, a former jet pilot, also believes in the existence of other beings and in the possibility that "flying saucers" are real. "Whatever you call them, they are real," concludes the senator. Author Israel Zangwill emphatically denounces "those smug astronomers, zoologists, and paleontologists who claim that man is alone in the universe. Scientists are not always right," was his assertion, and when he died in 1926 he had not changed his opinion.

For those who think that the subject is relatively new, I suggest an examination of the Bible. In Genesis we read of men from the sky meeting and mating with females on the earth. Biblical students may recall that Lot meets two angels who accompany him to his home, and in other sections of the Good Book we find many other allusions.

The *Book of Dzyan* in India tells of metal craft landing on the earth countless centuries ago. The visitors, we read, intermarried with the women of India and gradually were absorbed. We continue our reading to discover that the craft later took off from the earth, dropping an object which exploded in a way similar to that of an atomic bomb, causing overwhelming casualties on the earth.

Many of us have read of the terrible warlike craft seen over Ireland in the ninth century. One arrived at St. Kinaris Church in Cloers during Sunday mass with startling results. An anchor fluke caught under the eaves of the church, and while the assemblage waited in fear and with misgivings, a crew member came down the rope hand over hand and disengaged the fluke. Climbing back to the aircraft, he disappeared inside, whereupon the airship sailed away and was never seen again. It is said that the scar from the anchor, however, was still pointed out at the church during the last century.

Several years ago astronaut Gordon Cooper stated that although he didn't believe in fairy tales, "there have been far too many unexplained examples of UFO sightings around this earth for us to rule out the possibility that some form of life exists out there beyond our own world."

More than a year later Major Cooper was passing over Australia at a speed of 17,000 miles an hour on his fifteenth trip around the earth. Suddenly he radioed that a greenish object was approaching him from the opposite direction. He was then one hundred miles in the air. Meanwhile, on the ground, everyone at the Australian Muchea tracking station saw what Cooper described.

At Stanford University in California all that can be done

toward encouraging the goal of interworld communication is being carried out in cooperation with groups which include the Ames Research Center and the National Aeronautics and Space Administration. The organization, which has the alluring name of Cyclops, is attempting to establish that many intelligent "species" may have been active in the universe even before this world of ours was brought into being.

It is possible, suggests Cyclops, that eons ago there were efforts from other planets or worlds which could have begun an organized series of contacts of as yet unknown nature. These efforts or activities may have extended across galaxy after galaxy, available to civilizations which were able to bring together some type of workable plan or system of communication.

At the present time we on this globe have the ability to assemble equipment which theoretically can send signals to other galaxies. At Arecibo in Puerto Rico the gigantic radio telescope has the ability to signal millions and even trillions of miles away to beings who may have similar abilities to communicate, even if those to whom we wish to signal are living on other planets a thousand light years away.

Of course, the communication must be of a type simple enough yet complex enough to carry out our plans. We attempted it before with Project Ozma, when in 1960 we began to aim our efforts at star Tau Tauri and star Epsilon Eridant. However, although we spent about five hundred hours in our attempt, we were unable to find anything of which we could be absolutely sure.

Of course, there is another side to all of this, for we are told that the first actual interchange of communication between our world and any other intelligence might mean the termination of our "splendid isolation."

What some thinkers are said to fear is that an alien culture could pretend to teach us the superior ways of their own particular galaxies but in the process make us subservient to them without our realizing it. Then there are those who believe that even if that particular culture is far superior to ours, we would be reluctant to adopt it.

Opposing this type of thinking, the Cyclops group suggests that if we wait for other cultural beings to contact us, we may be too late. We are told that it is advisable to take the initiative.

While in the sixteenth, seventeenth, and eighteenth centuries discovery followed discovery in almost endless profusion, many learned men of today claim that we are unable to find frontiers "for geographic or cultural discoveries." They seem to ignore the uncharted frontiers of other worlds which are beckoning mysteriously to the earth-bound adventurers of this twentieth century.

Do we of this world have the right type of faith to go ahead and try to establish a system of thought interchange that will bring about understanding between our world and worlds in other galaxies? On the other hand, will our refusal to admit or accept the possibility that other intelligent beings can and do talk or exchange thoughts in one way or another limit us forever from interworld communication?

Time will tell.

PART 2

Monsters from Watery Abysses

1

Sea Monsters — 1751 to 1848

The subject of sea serpents and monsters of the deep has interested me for as long as I can remember. I probably have indulged in intense research on this subject for well over half a century, and when I read the words of Sherlock Holmes in Sir Arthur Conan Doyle's short story "Beryl Coronet," I decided that he had stated my ideas exactly. Holmes said that "when you have excluded the impossible, whatever remains, however improbable, must be the truth."

I also agree with René Bruyère in his *Caractères,* where he wrote that "there are disconcerting facts affirmed by serious men who have witnessed them or who have learnt of them from men like themselves." He goes on to say that to accept all or to deny all had "equal disadvantage." He suggests that, as in the ancient days when sailors were forced to guide their ships between the rock of Scylla and the whirlpool of Charybdis,* there is a course to be steered between "the credulous and the unbelievers."

*Homer mentions these two danger areas which are located between Italy and Sicily in the Straits of Messina.

James Fenimore Cooper once said that there is a reluctance in "the human mind to acknowledge that others have seen that which chance has concealed from our own sight."

It was well over half a century ago that Professor Leon Valliant of the French Museum of Natural History wrote that "the existence of the sea monster commonly known as the sea serpent is no longer in doubt today."

Now, in 1974, scores upon scores of scientific researchers, many of whom teach in colleges all over the world and many others who explore the sea bottom, agree with the professor. Down through the years scoffers and those who enjoy the pleasure of ridiculing their fellow men have confidently referred to those who believe in sea serpents as misinformed, mistaken, or downright liars. Now they maintain a respectful silence.

It was not so even three or four generations ago. Many scientific personalities of the past century often announced that because of their own superior knowledge they had decided that sea monsters and serpents never had lived, did not exist then, and never would exist in the future. Therefore, they said, the matter was settled as far as they were concerned and should never even be discussed by others.

My book *The Romance of Boston Bay,* published in 1944, contained a chapter concerning sea serpents. Letters which I received on the subject were many and varied. Some writers denounced me for being so unscientific as to consider the possible existence of these strange inhabitants of the deep, and others actually were sure that they had seen sea serpents with their own eyes.

Later, in writing *Mysteries and Adventures Along the Atlantic Coast** I told of still more experiences with strange inhabitants of our oceans, noting several additional instances

*Both books are now long out of print.

of man's encounter with these creatures. In ending my comments, I stated a wish that someday "the Sea Serpent will be . . . captured dead or alive, proving his existence to the doubters of the world."

Nonbelievers in his majesty the sea serpent usually claim that those who sight such objects are victims of overindulgence in intoxicating beverages, or, if such people are teetotalers, that they have seen one of the following: schools of porpoises, horse mackerel, seals, basking sharks, eels, giant squid, grampuses, masses of seaweed, water spouts, and killer whales. If the objects are proved to be none of these, then the people are said to have had optical illusions or to have suffered mass hallucinations. In other words, the scoffers and doubters will use any means at their disposal to discredit the most accurate observers who have ever sighted sea serpents.

Nevertheless, sea serpents have been well documented, as the following stories, some never before told, show.

A relatively large amount of publicity has been given both the Gloucester sea serpent and the Nahant sea serpent of the early nineteenth century in New England, but visits which the sea serpent or sea serpents made to Maine have been practically ignored by marine historians, if, indeed, they were aware of the incidents at all. We are fortunate, however, in having firsthand information on the entire series of incidents in Maine, actually written in the handwriting of those who saw the creature.*

The first recorded visit of the sea serpent to the shores of Maine was in 1751 when Joseph Kent of Marshfield, Maine, observed the creature from his eighty-five-ton sloop. Kent affirmed that the monster was "longer and larger" than the vessel's main boom and that he was able to see the serpent

*The author has copies of the original letters.

from a distance of forty feet. The creature was about forty-five feet long. The head, "which he carried four or five feet above the water," was nearly the size of that of a man. Kent was then in the vicinity of Muscongus, Maine.

In or about 1770 Captain Paul Reed of Boothbay saw a similar sea serpent. Captain Eleazar Crabtree noticed the monster in Penobscot Bay, Maine, around 1778, and estimated its length was sixty feet and its diameter the size of a barrel. He then lived at Fox Island, and the sea serpent appeared just offshore from the Crabtree residence on the island.

Crabtree went down to the water's edge to satisfy his own mind about what it might be. Indeed, it was a large sea serpent, about thirty rods from the shore, with its head about four feet out of water, and its length one hundred feet. Many other people on the island declared that they had noticed such a creature and that more than one of the serpents had been seen at the same time by several persons.

About 1779 Mr. Stephen Tuckey saw the sea serpent and stated that it was about fifty or sixty feet in length, as estimated by that portion of the creature which could be seen.

Captain George Little, who commanded the frigate *Boston,* wrote a letter concerning the sea serpent to the American Academy of Arts and Sciences, saying that he had been aboard a public armed ship lying in Round Pond below Broad Bay above Pemaquid Point when he saw a large sea serpent coming toward him. There were several men in the boat and he was about to have them fire at the creature, but the sea serpent submerged before the firing began. The creature came up again near Muscongus Island. Captain Little ordered the pursuit to continue, but the boat never came within a quarter mile of him again.

When the British were sailing to Castine during the Revolution, they sighted the sea serpent in Penobscot Bay, but

Sailors sight a phantom ship on the open sea. (Pt. I, Ch. 6)

Sea monster seen from the *Daedalus*. (Pt. II, Ch. 1)

Sea serpent "engraved from a drawing taken from Life as appeared in Gloutester Harbour, August 18, 1817." (Pt. II, Ch. 1)

Fight between sea serpent and sperm whale, seen from barque *Pauline,* from the *Illustrated London News,* 1875. (Pt. II, Ch. 4)

A sixteenth-century sea serpent, from Gesner's *Historiae Animalium,* 1551-87.

Looking into the mouth of an eighty-one-pound sea monster hooked by the author off Winthrop, Massachusetts.

Crowd at the monster site, 1970. (Pt. II, Ch. 6)

Strange head of the Mann Hill monster, found November 1970. (Pt. II, Ch. 6)

Hydrarchos sillimani, as exhibited by Dr. Albert Koch in 1845.

A Norwegian sea serpent seen in 1734.

Last sighting of Captain Herndon on the wheelhouse of the *Central America*. (Pt. III, Ch. 2)

The sinking of the *Central America*. (Pt. III, Ch. 2)

Undersea salvage work in the 1850s.

Loss of the *Royal George,* 1782. (Pt. IV, Ch. 1)

Unsuccessful salvage efforts on the *Royal George,* 1783.

Salvage attempts on the *Royal George,* 1841.

Preparations for the emergence of *Vasa* from the bottom. (Pt. IV, Ch. 1)

Putting preservative on ornaments from the *Vasa*.

Launching of the American submarine *Scorpion*. (Pt. IV, Ch. 3)

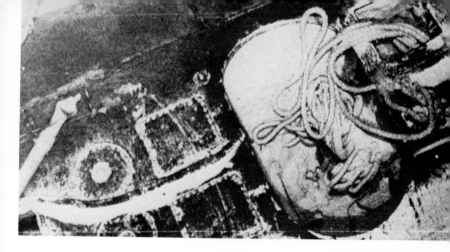

Scorpion wreckage, photographed on the bottom of the ocean.

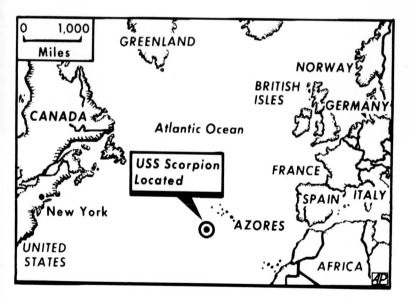

The submarine *Alvin,* which joined in the search for the *Scorpion.*

OPPOSITE TOP: Citizens watching the Boston Tea Party, December 16, 1773, from *Ballou's Pictorial Drawing-Room Companion,* 1856. (Pt. V, Ch. 3)

BOTTOM: View of the Boston Tea Party from *Ballou's Pictorial.*

Photo by Frederick G. S. Clow

Celebration of the Boston Tea Party on December 16, 1973, two hundred years after the event, with real tea saved from the original party. Left to right: James Douglass, Helen Salkowski, Edward Rowe Snow, Mrs. Snow, Arthur Cunningham.

their estimate of his length, three hundred feet, appears to be slightly exaggerated. People at Mount Desert Island also saw the monster at that time.

A Mr. Crockett evidently observed two sea serpents together about the year 1787.

A certain Mr. Miller of one of the Penobscot Bay Islands saw the sea serpent around 1785, as big as a ship's boom and about sixty to seventy feet long. In 1794 the inhabitants of Fox Island and Long Island, Maine, saw the sea serpent. Five years later two young men of Fox Island, "intelligent and credible," saw a sea serpent about sixty feet long, appearing "to have an ascending and descending motion."

On August 17, 1803, Abraham Cummings of Sullivan, Maine, in response to a request from John Quincy Adams, wrote out the details of his sight of the "extraordinary sea monster." He thought at first that it was a shoal of fish with a seal at one end, but on getting closer found it was a single animal in the form of a serpent.

> I immediately perceived that his mode of swimming was exactly such as had been described to me by some of the people at Fox Island, which must confirm the veracity of their report. For this creature had not the horizontal but an ascending and descending serpentine motion. This renders it highly probably that he never moves on land to any considerable distance and that the water is his proper element. His head was rather larger than that of a horse, but formed like that of a serpent. . . . His motion was at first moderate, but when he left us and proceeded toward the ocean, he moved with the greatest rapidity. This monster is the sixth of the kind, if our information be correct, which has been seen in this bay within the term of eighteen years.

Later Abraham Cummings added further details. "He had a serpent's head, of a colour as blue as possible, and a black ring around his eye."

Evidently Cummings had been questioned severely about part of his original letter and the suggestion was made that what he had seen were porpoises or whales. His answer follows:

Who ever saw fifty or sixty porpoises moving after each other in such a manner that those who formed the rear were no larger than haddock or mackerel, and none but the foremost shewed his head? Who ever saw a serpent's head upon a porpoise or a whale? We saw him swim as far as from Long Island to the Cape before he disappeared. His head and neck all the time out of water. Now who ever saw a porpoise swim so great a distance without ever emerging at all?

The Reverend Alden Bradford of Wiscasset, Maine, made a careful study of all the information he could obtain concerning the sea serpent. In a letter dated May 22, 1804, he spoke of the vague rumors of a sea serpent having been seen in or near Penobscot Bay. He went on to state that "little credit, however, was attached to the story." Nevertheless, he went ahead and collected information from the Reverend Alexander McLean, the Reverend Mr. Cummings of Sullivan, and Captain George Little of the frigate *Boston*. After his interviews with the three men he changed his opinion completely. "All this evidence," admitted the Reverend Mr. Bradford, "cannot fail to establish that a large sea serpent has been seen in and near the Bay of Penobscot."

After a lapse of several years sea serpents were again reported in New England. In June 1815 Captain Elkanah Finney of Plymouth, Massachusetts, was at work near his house at Warren's Cove, where "the beach joins the mainland." His son, whose name was not given, came from the shore and told Captain Finney "of an unusual appearance" in the water down at the cove. Captain Finney paid little attention to the boy's story at first, but as the lad persisted in telling his father about the unusual appearance, the captain eventually glanced down at the water and noticed something which appeared as "adrift seaweed."

Captain Finney then picked up his telescope and "in a moment" realized it was some "aquatic animal, with the form, motion and appearance of which I had hitherto been unacquainted."

The creature was about a quarter of a mile from shore, moving northward at a rapid speed. After traveling half a mile north, the animal turned about, appearing to be about one hundred feet long. Swimming toward Warren's Cove, the animal stopped and lay entirely still on the surface of the water. Captain Finney then had a good look at the monster of the deep.

The creature resembled a string of lobster buoys,

> perhaps thirty or forty of these protuberances or bunches, which were about the size of a barrel. The head appeared to be about six or eight feet long, and where it was connected with the body was a little larger than the body. His head tapered off to the size of a horse's head. I could not discern any mouth. But what I supposed to be his under jaw had a white stripe extending the whole length of the head, just above the water.

Captain Finney never did see the tail. The serpent's color was a deep black or brown. No view of eyes, mane, gills, or breathing holes was made, nor did Captain Finney hear a sound from the beast at any time.

When the visitation occurred, the sky was clear, the wind calm, and the water smooth. The sea serpent remained quiet for about five minutes and then moved away more slowly than at his former speed. He was soon out of sight.

The appearance of his majesty the sea serpent aroused the Finney household, and Captain Finney was up bright and early the next day to see if the serpent would reappear. Shortly after eight o'clock the creature was seen a mile down the beach in a northerly direction. For the next two hours the serpent disappeared and reappeared at intervals of five and ten minutes, after which he swam off toward the Gurnet Lighthouse. When questioned as to whether the motion of the sea serpent was up and down or right and left, Captain Finney could not answer, but did say that the fastest speed attained by the monster was fifteen or twenty miles an hour.

To make certain that his account of the remarkable creature would be believed, Captain Finney swore to the truth of the above statement before Justice of the Peace Nathaniel M. Davis in Plymouth on October 2, 1817.

In the month of August 1817 reports came of a sea serpent seen in Gloucester Harbor, Massachusetts. The first news came, strangely enough, from S. G. Perkins of Boston in a letter to his friend, Edward Everett, then in Paris. The letter, dated August 20, 1817, stated that "about a fortnight since, two women, who live near the entrance of the Harbour of Cape Ann, reported that they saw a Sea-Monster come into the Harbour, that it had the appearance of a Snake, was of great length."

On August 10, between twelve and one o'clock, Amos Story of Gloucester saw a strange marine animal, which he believed was a serpent, to the southward and eastward of Ten Pound Island. The sea serpent remained in view for one and a half hours and was within one hundred yards of Story. The head of the creature was like that of a sea turtle, larger than that of any dog Story had ever seen, and the serpent carried the head from ten to twelve inches above the surface of the water. Sixteen years later Amos Story became keeper at Ten Pound Island Light, and he never forgot his experience with his majesty the sea serpent.

The entire seaside around Gloucester was soon looking for the sea serpent, and it was not long before other reports came in.

Solomon Allen III was a Gloucester shipmaster. On August 12, 1817, he saw what he believed to be a sea serpent in Gloucester Harbor, about 150 yards away. The creature was estimated to be from eighty to ninety feet in length, about the size of a half barrel, and apparently having joints from his head to his tail. His cranium was formed "something like the head of the rattlesnake, but nearly as large as the head of a horse." When the sea serpent moved on the surface of the water, his motion was slow, at times playing about in circles, and sometimes swimming "nearly straight forward."

When the sea serpent disappeared, he apparently went right down to the bottom, and would next come to the surface about two hundred yards from the place where he vanished. The color of the creature was dark brown. Mr. Allen saw the serpent also on the two following days, according to a statement he made later before Coroner Lonson Nash, who served as justice of the peace in Essex County.

On August 14, 1817, Epes Ellery saw the serpent in Gloucester Harbor at a distance of 300 yards. Ellery saw the upper part of the head and about forty feet of the animal whose joints were about the size of a two-gallon keg. The serpent opened its jaws, revealing a mouth similar to that of a snake, and the top of his head was flat. When he swam "the first part of the curve that he made in turning was one of the form of a staple, and as he approached toward his tail, he came near his body with his head, and then ran parallel with his tail, and his head and tail then appeared together."

Matthew Gaffney, a ship carpenter of Gloucester, also sighted the sea serpent the same day between four and five in the afternoon and from a distance of thirty feet. His head was the size of a "four-gallon keg, his body as large as a barrel, and his length that I saw, I should judge, forty feet at least." The top of his head was dark in color, and the underside of his head nearly white, as were also several feet of his belly.

> I fired at him [stated Matthew Gaffney] when he was the nearest to me. I had a good gun and took good aim. I aimed at his head and think I must have hit him. He turned toward us immediately after I had fired, and I thought he was coming at us; but he sunk down and went directly under our boat, and made his appearance at about one hundred yards from where he sank. He did not turn down like a fish, but appeared to settle directly down, like a rock. My gun carries a ball of eighteen to a pound, and I suppose there is no person in town more accustomed to shooting than I am. I have seen the animal at several other times, but never so good a view of him as on this day. His motion was vertical, like a caterpillar.

Matthew Gaffney also stated that the creature swam twenty to thirty miles an hour and was able to turn rapidly and in a small space, so that his head and tail "appear almost to touch each other." Daniel Gaffney and Augustin M. Webber were also in the boat with Matthew at the time of the incident.

Lonson Nash saw the creature on August 14 and described the monster's movement as vertical, saying that he believed the serpent to be straight, with "the apparent bunches," of which he saw eight, "caused by his vertical motion." He estimated the speed of the serpent swimming in the water to be about a mile in four minutes. Nash thought that the creature was seventy feet long at least, though he would not be surprised if the animal measured one hundred feet.

James Mansfield of Gloucester sighted the serpent on August 15, 1817, and believed the length of the creature to be from forty to sixty feet, but stated that the bunches were still in evidence when the serpent lay still in the water. In this he disagreed with Lonson Nash, who stated that the bunches appeared only when the creature was in motion.

Three days later, on August 18, William B. Pearson of Gloucester was in a sailboat off Webber's Cove with James P. Collins, when the sea serpent swam out under the stern of their craft. They both cried out, "Here is the snake!" The creature was at least seventy feet long, and they noticed "bunches on his back." The sea serpent swam by the bow of the sailboat ninety feet away. His color was dark brown and his motion was vertical. Pearson was also nearby the day Gaffney fired at the monster and thought that Gaffney hit the creature on that occasion.

No less a personality than the eminent Colonel Thomas Handasyd Perkins visited Gloucester for the express purpose of viewing the sea serpent, and after satisfying himself "that the report in circulation was not a fable," sat on a point of land which projected into the harbor. "Whilst thus seated," wrote Colonel Perkins, "I observed an agitation in the water at the entrance of the harbour, like that which follows a small vessel going five or six miles an hour through the water. As we knew there was no shoal where the water was thus broken, I immediately said to Mr. Lee that I had no doubt that what I had seen was the sea serpent in pursuit of fish."

Colonel Perkins estimated that he saw about forty feet of

the serpent's body, which was of a "chocolate colour." The sea serpent's head was flat, but something "like a single horn, about nine inches to a foot in length, and of the form of a marlinspike" could be seen in the front part of the head.

Colonel Perkins also interviewed a gentleman named Mansfield whose wife saw the creature with him on August 18, 1817. He and his wife agreed that the serpent was about one hundred feet long and stretched out "partly over the white sandy beach, which had four or five feet of water upon it, and lay partly over the channel."

At another occasion the serpent was seen on the rocky shore at Ten Pound Island, "resting partly on the rocks, and partly in the water."

The next important report we include came from a point about two miles out to sea from Cape Ann where Sewall Toppan, captain of the schooner *Laura*, was becalmed at nine in the morning of August 28, 1817. He heard one of the crew exclaim and ask what it was that was coming toward them, but he was busy and paid no attention immediately. After a few moments Captain Toppan climbed on the deck load to see "a singular kind of animal or fish, which I had never before seen, passing by our quarter at a distance of about forty feet, standing along shore." The creature was dark in color, and the head appeared to be the size of a ten-gallon keg and had something which resembled a tongue, according to William Somerby and Robert Bragg, crewmen aboard the *Laura*. The motion of the head was sideways while the motion of the body was up and down. "I have been to sea many years," concluded Captain Toppan, "and never saw any fish that had the least resemblance to this animal."

Bragg stated that the serpent swam within twenty-eight or thirty feet of the *Laura*,

passing very swiftly by us; he left a long wake behind us ... he threw out his tongue about two feet in length; the end of it appeared to me to resemble a fisherman's harpoon; he raised his tongue several times perpendicularly, or nearly so, and let it fall again . . . his back and body appeared smooth; a small bunch was on each side of his head, just above his eyes; he did not appear to be disturbed by the vessel; his course was in the direction for the Salt Islands.

Somerby saw one of the creature's eyes, which "appeared very bright, about the size of the eye of an ox." He said that the serpent "threw his tongue backwards several times over his head, and let it fall again." Somerby claimed that the meeting took place off Brace's Cove.

The sea serpent evidently tired of the vicinity about this time, for when we hear of him next he is in Long Island Sound, New York, where Thomas Herttell of Rye Neck saw him on October 15, 1817. The location was a short distance from his house, just offshore from Mr. Ezekiel Halsted's dwelling on Rye Point. He saw a long, rough, dark-looking body moving toward New York up the Sound against a brisk wind and a strong ebb tide. "That it is what is usually called a Sea-Serpent, and the same which appeared in Gloucester Harbor, is only probable."

On June 6, 1819, Captain Hawkins Wheeler of Fairfield, Connecticut, while aboard the sloop *Concord* off Race Point, Massachusetts, saw the sea serpent one hundred yards away. The head resembled that of a snake and was from four to seven feet above the water. His back apparently was

composed of bunches or humps . . . a little larger than half a barrel; I think I saw as many as ten or twelve, but did not count them; I considered them to be caused by the undulatory motion of the animal—the tail was not visible, but from the head to the last hump that could be seen, was, I should judge, fifty feet. The first view I had of him appeared like a string of empty barrels tied together, rising over what little swell of the sea there was.

Nahant, Massachusetts, was the next port of call for this unusual New England sea serpent. The first report from this region was from a Mr. Smith, who told Marshal James Prince that vast numbers of people were at Nahant Beach, where the sea serpent had been sighted on August 12, 1819, the day before the interview. Marshal Prince hurried down to the shore and was fortunate in seeing the serpent a short time after he arrived. Having his "masthead spy-glass" with him, he made a careful observation.*

"His head appeared about three feet out of water," recorded Marshal Prince. "I counted thirteen bunches on his back; my family thought there were fifteen—he passed three times at a moderate rate across the bay, but so fleet as to occasion a foam in the water—and my family and myself, who were in the carriage, judged he was fifty feet in length."

Mrs. Prince and the coachman had much better vision than the marshal and were of great assistance in helping him observe the creature in the water. On one occasion when the sea serpent came in closer than at any other time, the coachman remarked, "Oh, see his glistening eye!" Two or three hundred persons observed him at Nahant that day, including among others Samuel Cabot, James Magee, fisherman John Marston of Swampscott and Thomas Handasyd Perkins.

Marston, a veteran sailor who was quite familiar with all of the regular animals and fish along the coast—seals, porpoises, sharks, horse mackerel and smaller and larger fish of

*Marshal James Prince was the officer whose duty it was to execute many pirates in Boston. I mention him in my book *True Tales of Pirates and Their Gold.*

all varieties—said that he had never seen anything like it before.

Samuel Cabot, great-great-great grandfather of Henry Cabot Lodge, said that he saw eight to ten "bunches or protuberances, and at a short interval, three or four more."

On August 26, 1819, Chaplain Cheever Felch was on board the schooner *Science,* then engaged in surveying off the Massachusetts coast. Others in the party included William T. Malbone and Midshipman Blake. While proceeding down Gloucester Harbor, Chaplain Felch saw the sea serpent about thirty or forty yards away. The creature went down at once, rose again within twenty yards of the *Science,* lay for some time on the water, and then headed in the direction of Ten Pound Island. The schooner followed him and then launched a boat, but the creature evidently objected to the noise of the oars, so the men laid them in and sculled the boat.

Again they drew closer to the serpent. The creature continued to play between Ten Pound Island and Stage Point or the Fort, whereupon the men landed at the Fort, sending a messenger to the schooner to inquire as to what effect a twelve-pound carronade might have on the creature. Cheever counted fourteen bunches on his back, "the first one, say ten or twelve feet from his head, and the others about seven feet apart. They decreased in size toward the tail. These bunches were sometimes counted with, and sometimes without, a glass. Mr. Malbone counted thirteen, Mr. Blake thirteen and fourteen and the boatman about the same number. . . . Mr. Malbone, until this day, was incredulous. No man would now convince him there was not such a being."

The last account important enough to be mentioned in our chapter concerns the officers of the British corvette H.M.S. *Daedalus,* who, while sailing on the ocean in the afternoon of August 6, 1848, saw a sea serpent in latitude 24°44'S and in longitude 9°22'E. As this incident is still available in other publications, I am not going to give too detailed an account.

It was five in the afternoon when the midshipman on duty, Satoris by name, noticed the serpent and immediately reported the fact to the officer of the watch, Lieutenant Edgar A. Drummond. At the time Captain Peter M'Quhae, who later probably wished he had never made an official report of the incident, was walking the quarterdeck with the navigating officer, Mr. William Barrett. The ship's company were at supper.

"On our attention being called to the object it was discovered to be an enormous serpent, with head and shoulders kept about four feet constantly above the surface of the sea," reported Captain M'Quhae. He went on to say that at least sixty feet of the being was showing in the water. "It passed rapidly, but so close under our lee quarter, that had it been a man of my acquaintance I should have recognized his features easily with the naked eye. . . . The diameter of the serpent was about fifteen or sixteen inches behind the head, which was, without any doubt, that of a snake, and it was never, during the twenty minutes that it continued in sight of our glasses, once below the surface of the water."

For the first time in history, man's attention was focused on the problem of the existence of the sea serpent by its official appearance in a government report from a battleship at sea. The usual number of disbelievers soon presented themselves and were strongly seconded by many of the scientific personalities of the day.

Sir Richard Owen, a great man in many ways with an almost superhuman capacity for investigation, often gave proof of a "singular and not entirely scientific type of mind." His attack on Darwin's theory of man was not as radical as his complete refusal to accept the *Daedalus* story. This scientific genius, head of England's Hunterian Museum, stated that "a larger body of evidence might be got together in proof of ghosts than of the sea serpent."

Owen also wrote a letter to the London *Times*. This recognized expert had a worldwide reputation as a naturalist and paleontologist, and his message to the *Times* was one of the longest letters I have ever read in that illustrious paper— nearly a column. Excerpts follow.

I am far from insensible to the pleasures of the discovery of a new and rare animal, but before I can enjoy them certain conditions, e.g., reasonable proof or evidence of its existence, must be fulfilled. . . . It is very probable that no one on board the *Daedalus* ever before beheld a gigantic seal freely swimming in the open ocean. . . . In other words, I regard the negative evidence . . . as stronger than the positive statements which have hitherto weighed with the public mind.

Captain M'Quhae was quick to reply, and again I quote from the London *Times*.

I now assert—neither was it a common seal nor a sea elephant, its great length and its totally differing physiognomy precluding the possibility of its being a "Phoca" of any species. The head was flat, and not a "capacious vaulted cranium"; nor had it a "stiff inflexible trunk"—a conclusion to which Professor Owen has jumped, most certainly not justified by the simple statement, that "no portion of the 60 feet seen by us was used in propelling it through the water, either by vertical or horizontal undulation." . . . Finally I deny the existence of excitement, or the possibility of optical illusion. I adhere to the statement, as to form, colour, and dimensions, contained in my official report to the Admiralty.

Actually, in all fairness to M'Quhae, Owen often distorted facts to conform with his own theories. Eventually, Owen's dismissal of M'Quhae's sea monster failed to win any measure of acceptance among scientists and naturalists in general.

R. A. Proctor in his *Pleasant Ways in Science* gives the following comments:

> It might be probable enough that no one on board the *Daedalus* had ever seen a gigantic seal freely swimming in the open ocean—a sight which Professor Owen himself had certainly never seen—yet we could hardly suppose they would not have known a sea-elephant under such circumstances. . . . No one could mistake a sea-elephant for any other living creature, even though his acquaintance with the animal were limited to museum specimens or pictures in books.
>
> The supposition that the entire animal, that is, its entire length should be mistaken for 30 or 40 feet of the length of a serpentine neck, seems, in my judgment, as startling as the ingenious theory thrown out by some naturalists when they first heard of the giraffe—to the effect that someone of lively imagination had mistaken the entire body of a short-horned antelope for the neck of a much larger animal!

In thinking about the existence of sea serpents, it is well to keep in mind the story of the ancient resident of a small town near Rutland, Vermont. He had never seen a train and doubted its existence. Finally his friends took him to see one. His first remark was that it wouldn't start. Then, when it did, he stated that it wouldn't stop. The story probably applies to most doubters of the sea serpent, if and when they see one.

2

A Significant Occurrence

On October 1, 1850, the whaling ship *Monongahela* sailed away from New Bedford bound for the North Pacific. Three months before this her master, Captain Jason Seabury, had brought the *Monongahela* from Philadelphia to New Bedford.*

As Captain Seabury watched the New Bedford seaport fade away behind him, little did he realize how much his ship would contribute to the settlement of a worldwide controversy hundreds of years old.

The weeks aboard ship sped by. On the morning of January 13, 1852, the *Monongahela* was in the Pacific, cruising along in latitude 3°10'S and longitude 131°50'W, a few hundred miles from the Marquesas Islands. She was sailing in company with the four-hundred-ton *Rebecca Sims,* whose master was Samuel B. Gavitt.

Nothing of unusual interest was taking place at the time, when suddenly "the man on the lookout, seated on the fore

*The *Monongahela* had been built in Philadelphia in 1828.

topmast crosstrees" shouted out at the top of his voice.

"White water!"

"Where away?" came the captain's reply.

"Two points on the lee bow."

Everyone supposed that the disturbance in the water was made by sperm whales, and, being extremely anxious to obtain oil, Captain Seabury ordered the ship to be kept off and went aloft with his own spyglass.

Previously the *Monongahela* had been struggling along for several days with "very light and baffling winds," but at daylight of the morning of the thirteenth the wind had drawn to the south southwest, becoming steady and then threatening to develop into a gale.

Captain Seabury remained aloft with his telescope for more than half an hour before he noticed white water and decided that the disturbance was created by a school of porpoises rather than sperm whales. He was inclined to forget the incident, but "wishing to be certain," he ordered the mate, "as it was seven bells, to turn all hands, square in the yards, and send out the port studding sails."

Captain Seabury then went below for breakfast, but before he could begin his meal, he heard a shrill cry from Onnetu Vanjan, a Marquesas islander.

"Oh, look! Look! Me see, too much, too much!"

The captain rushed out on deck and looked in the direction the islander was pointing just in time to see "black skin" disappearing off the lee quarter. Captain Seabury hurried over to Onnetu.

"What was it, Onnetu? What did you see? Tell me fast, Onnetu!"

"No whale, no, sir! No, much too big, too long. Me no see all same that fellow. Me afraid!"

The captain gave orders to luff and return to the approximate position, meanwhile ordering the lines in the boats and

the crews to stand by. Everyone aboard stood looking seaward in all directions for nearly an hour, and then as nothing
unusual appeared, Captain Seabury ordered the attempt
abandoned and went below again to eat.

Onnetu received some friendly bantering but took it all in
good grace, for he knew that what he had sighted was indeed
a strange monster of the deep. After all, even the captain had
been able to see the glistening black skin as the creature
disappeared, and to this argument, which Onnetu advanced,
the scoffers had no answer.

Onnetu continued to scan the ocean carefully, refusing to
move away from his post even for the call of breakfast. Then
he saw the monster again, but Onnetu decided to do nothing
about it until he was sure. A moment later the being pulled
itself out of the water in such magnificence that Onnetu
could no longer keep from shouting.

"Look, look!" came his shrill voice even louder than the
first time, and now his cry electrified the entire ship. "Onnetu
make no mistake. No whale. Big, too long. Look, look!"

All hands ran on deck, and sure enough, Onnetu was
vindicated. Captain Seabury could now easily see the creature at a distance of about three-quarters of a mile to the
leeward. This was the strangest being that Captain Seabury
had ever observed, the body resembling a gigantic weaving
rope, several feet in diameter, while the head was concealed
for the moment.

Captain Seabury ordered the ship to approach the creature, and as the *Monongahela* neared the being, all hands
could hear the strange, sobbing noise which it emitted as its
body continued to weave in and out in unusual fashion, "like
the waving of a rope, when shaken and held in the hand."

Every person on board watched the creature, and not a
word was spoken. A few minutes later, to the amazement of
all, the entire twisting body, unbelievably long and gigantic

in size, came into view. Within a few minutes the tail began to vibrate, and the head rose slowly out of the sea, moving sideways as "if the monster was in agony or suffocating." Captain Seabury was almost overcome by the realization that they were actually staring at a sea serpent.

"It is a sea serpent," he exclaimed. "Stand by the boats."

For Captain Seabury had suddenly become obsessed with an idea—to capture the creature and bring it home for all doubters to see, and because they had seen, to believe as well. But the mate was hesitant.

"Of what use is there lowering for him? We'd only lose time and gain nothing besides."

Captain Seabury checked the mate at once. "Never mind that sort of talk. Call all hands aft!"

When the crew was mustered aft the captain addressed them. "We've got something here which will make history. I wish to try* this fellow. Every man of you knows that few people believe that the creature you're looking at even exists. I've often heard it expressed that a whale ship might capture one of these creatures some day, and now is our chance. You know what'll happen when we return home and try to tell others that we saw the sea serpent. You know the smiles we'll get. But what can they do if we bring the sea serpent back with us? You know the answer just as well as I do. And if we don't bring him back they'll say right off, 'Why didn't you try him?' Our courage is at stake, even our manhood, and it might be said the whole American whaling fishery. Think what it would mean if we brought the sea serpent into some southern port!"

The captain paused, allowed the speech to sink in just a little, and then went on talking.

"I do not order even one of you to go in the boats. On the other hand, who will volunteer?"

*A whaling term which means to separate the oil from the blubber.

Every American seaman on board stepped forward, and all the others except one native and two from Britain. The captain had won his point. He now ordered the boat steerers and his officers to examine all gear and see that everything in and about the boats was in perfect order.

Captain Seabury had already leaped into his boat when the sea serpent started moving through the water, necessitating the ship's standing after him. Jumping back aboard the ship, the captain continued to carry sail, although the wind "was piping up strongly."

Working to windward, the serpent caused Captain Seabury to "haul on the wind," and soon afterward the *Monongahela* carried away her fore topgallant mast. This was extremely unlucky, but what was worse, the sea serpent disappeared. Repairs were made rapidly, and Captain Seabury still kept on the wind, hoping to see "his snake-ship" again.

Less than an hour passed before the sea serpent was sighted, swimming slowly along in the gathering windstorm. Then he turned in the water and headed abaft the *Monongahela*'s beam, so Captain Seabury put the ship on the other tack. By now the wind was almost gale force, and a single reef was put in the fore and mizzen topsails. The sea serpent disappeared again about this time, but was seen shortly afterward a mile ahead of the ship, having made a complete circuit to pass slowly to leeward.

By now Captain Seabury's hopes of capturing the sea serpent were very feeble, and the gale then blowing made him extremely hesitant about lowering. Nevertheless, as the *Monongahela* came up with the creature, the sea serpent lay still in the water. When the ship was less than half a mile to windward, she came to with the head yards aback to have a better control of all the ship.

Captain Seabury was now ready to lower. In the other two boats were the second mate and the first mate, both ready to lower the moment their commander gave the order.

"Shipkeeper," he called out, "keep close to us and by no means lose sight of us for an instant."

Seabury lowered first and the others followed. Then came the trip through the water. The wind and the sea carried the boats rapidly to leeward, and Captain Seabury soon was near the monster. It was a comparatively short time before the captain ordered his boat steerer, James Whittemore of Vermont, to prepare for the blow.

Whittemore stood up. He was calm and cool as he grasped the harpoon iron, and when the boat was close by the sea serpent, the captain made a motion with his hand.

The harpoon whistled through the air and buried itself in the body of its target. A second harpoon flashed and did likewise. Both weapons were buried to the socket in the body of the monstrous creature they were attempting to kill. Expecting a terrific commotion from the sea serpent, Captain Seabury shouted, "Stern," but there was no visible movement from their prey. The captain shifted places with the boat steerer and had cleared away a lance when the serpent made a slight movement, followed by a greater one. The two ends of the monster of the deep now appeared to be seeking out the wounds caused by the harpoons.

The frightfulness of the gigantic head as it swung around toward the harpoon thrusts and neared the occupants of the boat filled every member of the crew with terror. Three of them leaped into the sea to escape apparent death in the serpent's great crunching jaws. Captain Seabury stood up with his lance, and, as the hideous, giant head of the monster neared the boat, Seabury threw his lance directly into the gleaming eye, and for a split second saw the lance enter the eyeball.

The next thing Captain Seabury knew he was in the water, evidently knocked into the sea by the head of the colossal creature as it swung around. Rising to the surface, Seabury caught a brief glimpse of the writhing snake before he was struck again and carried below. This time he descended so far that he could feel himself losing consciousness, but when his lungs could stand no more he broke surface again and recovered enough to take a deep breath.

Meanwhile, the first mate and the second mate were maneuvering their own boats to come to the aid of Captain Seabury and his men. The captain took in the situation with a glance. He could see that the ocean was foaming and red from the three strikes which had been made into the serpent's body, but the wounded monster had disappeared again. Still treading water, he shouted across to the third mate, "Pick up the line."

Mr. Benson caught a bight of the captain's line and bent on his own, which immediately began to be taken out in rapid fashion. At the same time the captain and the three others were pulled from the water. One of the sailors was badly bruised, while another was unconscious.

By this time the sea serpent had taken the captain's line, the third mate's line, and was taking the second mate's line when the captain ordered the mate to bend on and give his line to the ship. The watersnake was sounding, and Captain Seabury cautioned the others not to hold on too hard for fear of drawing the irons from the monster's body. At first the line went out just as rapidly as the others had, but gradually the rate decreased. Nevertheless, Captain Seabury was obliged to get out a spare line from the forehold and bend on.

For fear that the ship would draw the irons by its own weight, Seabury put on several drags and gave the line to the mate, who released it into the sea. It became stationary. Four boat's lines were out now, 225 fathoms in a boat, and two-thirds of another line—in all no less than one thousand fathoms, one mile and an eighth! It was an enormous depth to which the creature had descended, and the pressure at that depth is inconceivable to the average person.

Meanwhile, not only had the wind kept up, but it had increased in force. Captain Seabury hardly dared to carry sail enough to keep the ship up. The boat was in peril, and the captain was obliged to take the line to the ship again and run the risk of the irons' drawing. The end of the line was made fast to the ship, and all sail, except enough to hold the *Monongahela* steady, was taken in.

Every man now awaited in alarm the moment when the sea serpent would rise to the surface again. They all wondered if the lines would part.

The wind, which had been extremely fierce most of the afternoon, began to shift around four o'clock, and by five had diminished greatly. Six o'clock passed. The men went to supper and finished their meal. Seven o'clock brought no change, nor did the hour of eight. Captain Seabury now went aboard his vessel.

Shortly before nine o'clock that night the line grew taut again. The weather was then ideal, the night a beautiful one, the sky clear with hardly a breath of air, and the sea falling. The line remained taut for the next few hours. At four o'clock the following morning, sixteen hours after the monster had sounded, the line began to slacken.

Captain Seabury ordered the line taken in on the windlass, and it was not until they had aboard two full lines hand over hand when there was a further strain. As this strain continued, Captain Seabury ordered everyone to "bear a hand and get breakfast." In the middle of the meal the cook appeared.

"There he is, sir."

There was a rush for the side, and sure enough, the sea serpent had risen to the surface, but all that was visible was a curved fragment of the body of the creature, evidently that part which had been struck with the harpoons.

Captain Seabury ordered all hands over the side, and they lanced the body repeatedly without the least signs of life. While this was going on, the creature's body gradually appeared on the surface. Around the monster's great form there floated what were apparently pieces of the serpent's lungs, and the men tried to find the heart of the creature in order to inflict the final death blow.

Suddenly the monster drew himself up, and all boats pulled away. The men were about to witness the terrific dying struggles of a sea serpent. No one who watched that fantastic event ever forgot it. The evolutions of the body became faster and faster until the movements were like lightning, resembling a "thousand enormous black wheels" turning at incredible speed. The tail and the head would occasionally appear in the surging bloody foam.

Then there came from the dying creature a sound so unearthly, so expressive of acute agony and so piercing, that a thrill of horror passed through the captain's body. From that moment the efforts of the serpent appeared to diminish, and fifteen minutes later all convulsive motion stopped completely. The sea serpent raised its great, horrible head a little out of water, appeared to glance at the men on the ship with its remaining good eye, and then the head slumped down into the water and the creature moved no more. It was dead. Every man gave rousing cheers for the remarkable victory over the denizen of the deep.

The dead serpent was buoyant and lay on the surface of the ocean. Slowly the inert body rolled over on its belly, and the crew cheered again.

The captain now held a consultation with the crew. It was agreed that the creature was too large to save in its entirety, but it was decided that the skin, the head, and the bones should be taken back to the United States.

One member of the crew who came from Scotland had been successful as an artist, and to him was entrusted the job of drawing sketches of the sea serpent before it was cut up. The next task was to measure it. Since the sea was now smooth, the work was easily carried out. The monster was found to be a male, one hundred three feet, seven inches long. It was nineteen feet, one inch around the neck and twenty-four feet, six inches around what the mate called the shoulders. The largest part of the body, probably the stomach, was forty-nine feet, eleven inches.

The sea serpent's head was long and flat with ridges. The bones of the lower jaw separated, and the end of the tongue was like the head of a heart. The tail ran nearly to a point, on the end of which was a firm, flat cartilage. The back was black, turning brown on the sides, then yellow, and on the center of the belly was a narrow white streak which ran two-thirds the length of the body. Dark spots were scattered over the entire skin.

There were two spout holes, or spiracles, indicating that the creature evidently breathed like a whale. It also had four swimming paws, or imitations of swimming paws, for they were like hard flesh.

The joints of the back were loose, and it seemed as if when it was swimming it moved two ribs and a joint at a time, "almost like feet." The muscular action of the creature after death made the body look as though it were encircled by longitudinal ridges.

When the head was taken in, it presented a frightful sight, and efforts were made to preserve it intact in salt. In the jaw there were ninety-four teeth as large as a man's thumb, deeply and firmly set and very sharp, pointing backward. All the bones of the creature, which appeared to be porous and dark colored, were saved. When the serpent was opened up, pieces of squid and a large blackfish were found inside. As soon as the blackfish was moved the flesh dropped off its bones. Captain Seabury preserved the serpent's heart in liquor and also saved the good eye.

The body of the serpent was covered with blubber resembling that of a whale, but the blubber was only four inches thick. The sea serpent was cut in, as the whaler's expression goes, but they found great difficulty with him, having to flense* him, for not only were they unable to roll the body, but the blubber was so elastic that a piece twenty feet long stretching on the blocks would shrink to five or six feet when cut off. The oil was clear as water and burned nearly as fast "as spirits of turpentine."

The men were nearly three days in getting the bones on board the *Monongahela.* Of course, Captain Seabury could not return to port without a paying load of whale oil, regardless of his desire to announce to the world his capture of the sea serpent, and so he sent the ten barrels of sea serpent oil back to New Bedford by another ship, along with seventy-three barrels of sperm oil and a packet of letters. The sea serpent oil was eventually used to illuminate many of the lighthouses of Boston Bay.

Aboard the whaleship *Rebecca Sims,* which I have already mentioned as cruising along with the *Monongahela* at the time of the capture of the serpent, was Alonzo D. Sampson, boat steerer, who later wrote of his experiences in *Three Times Around the World.* I quote pertinent excerpts from his book at this time:

We were cruising in company with the *Monongahela* of New Bedford, when the lookout at our masthead discovered a strange looking object in the water half a mile astern, and hailed with the intelligence. The Cap-

*A whaling term meaning to strip the blubber and skin from the creature.

tain was called and came on deck with his glass, and after examining the object he pronounced it an immense serpent. By this time we were all gathered on deck watching the motions of the monster, which would occasionally elevate its head to a height of some ten feet above the water, and after taking a survey of things would subside again to the surface. The Captain called for volunteers to capture the sea serpent. . . . The *Monongahela* was nearest to our game, but the two boats reached its vicinity at about the same time. The serpent lay quiet, only raising its head and looking around as eyeing first one boat and then the other. . . . I took my harpoon and launched it into the animal at about his middle, the steerer of the *Monongahela*'s boat doing the same thing on the other side at about the same moment. . . . The serpent began to writhe and go through the contortions usual with his kind, lashing the water furiously. . . . During his struggles there was a constant and singular change in color passing over the surface of the monster's body. He settled down on the spot . . . and so remained for the next twenty-four hours. . . . At the end of that period he came to the surface, dead. . . . The head, which was shaped like an alligator's, was ten feet long. . . . It had two small fins on each side of the body not far from the head; but its tail was that of a snake, pointed and without fins. . . . The bones were cleaned and stowed away, and we calculated upon settling the sea serpent question at rest. But it was fated otherwise. The *Monongahela* entered the northern seas in the spring and was lost; all hands perished. No vestige of the wreck was ever found except a cask or two.

It was one of the strangest jests of fate which prevented the *Monongahela* from returning to New Bedford with the skeleton and parts of the body of the sea serpent preserved in casks. Unfortunately, after his victory over the monster of the deep, Captain Seabury sailed for the northern Pacific, and his ship disappeared. Months passed without news of her, and then the report came that she had entered the Arctic Ocean in 1853. A cask was later picked up in the Arctic which had the private markings of the *Monongahela,* and in November, 1854, it was agreed that "there is little doubt that the vessel and her entire crew are lost."

What details were known were published in the Washington *Union* of November 29, 1855, where it was announced that the ship "was supposed to be lost on the Fox Islands in the autumn of 1853, as when she was last seen she was attempting to make her way through the 'seventy-second passage' (as it is termed), in longitude 172 degrees West, the wind at that time blowing a gale."

The Navy sent Acting Lieutenant William Gibson in command of the schooner *Fenimore Cooper* to search for possible survivors, and on reaching the Choumagne group of islands Lieutenant Gibson learned from Russian Governor Veovodsky that a vessel had been lost in the fall of 1853 near the Aleutian island of Atka. The Russian American Company's brig *Ochtotsck* had found the quarterboard of the *Monongahela,* which was sent back to New Bedford.

Years later Curator William Henry Tripp of the Old Dartmouth Historical Society in the Bourne Whaling Museum discovered the quarterboard in the attic of the old First National Bank Building in New Bedford, where it had evidently remained for many years. He reported his find to the relatives of Captain Seabury, Miss Sarah E. Seabury and Miss Caroline O. Seabury, who later presented the quarterboard to the Old Dartmouth Historical Society at the Bourne Whaling Museum. It now hangs on the walls there, a grim reminder of the only sea serpent ever captured.

Curator Tripp was greatly interested in my search for the facts about the *Monongahela* and capture of the sea serpent. When I visited him with my family in 1954 he told me of the return of the *Rebecca Sims* to this country to report the sea serpent story, and showed us the actual handwriting of Captain Seabury describing the incident. William Tripp stated emphatically that "without question the *Monongahela* sighted and captured a real sea serpent. It is unfortunate that she herself was lost before returning home."

How lucky it is that the letters sent back to the United States told the remarkable story of the battle with the sea serpent, the outstanding description couched in the almost forgotten language of the whalers.

3

The Sea Serpent World
of Parson Wood

About a century ago, across the sea in England, a preacher
named John George Wood became an ardent student in the
general field of marine inhabitants. Fascinated with the subject of sea serpents specifically, the Reverend Mr. Wood
began collecting every scrap of information he could find
about these strange denizens of the deep.

After journeying to New England, where he thought an
extremely fertile ocean area existed, Wood began as careful
a research project as ever was carried out in Massachusetts.
As a result, in the June 1884 issue of the *Atlantic Monthly*
he gives a truly delightful account of what he discovered
concerning the sea monster in the New England area.

Let us join the Reverend Mr. John George Wood in 1884
as he studies the case of a sea monster of the year 1823.
Luckily, Mr. Wood was able to interview an actual observer
of the 1823 incident sixty-one years after the occurence. The
preacher was intrigued with the possibility of a man-to-man
discussion of that event, and he went to Swampscott, Massa-

chusetts, where he met and interviewed Francis Johnson. He reported as follows:

> Mr. Francis Johnson testified that on July 12, 1823, his attention was struck by an object moving into the harbor [Swampscott] from Nahant, but, thinking it to be a row of porpoises, he did not trouble himself about it.
>
> "About two hours afterward [he said], I heard a noise in the water, and saw about four rods distant something resembling the head of a fish or serpent elevated about two feet above the surface, followed by seven or eight bunches, the first about six feet from the head, all about six feet apart, and raised about six inches above the water."
>
> He pursued it for half an hour, and was in full sight of it all the time. On landing, Mr. Johnson made a statement of his experience before six gentlemen, all of whom could vouch for his integrity. Happily, although this event occurred so long ago, Mr. Johnson is still living [April 7, 1884] and can speak for himself.
>
> There is a casual mention of the sea serpent as having made another Norwegian appearance in 1822, but no one appears to have seen it on the New England shore until 1826, when it again appeared off Nahant, as it is recorded very briefly in the Lynn *Mirror*.
>
> Seven years elapsed, and again the animal appeared in its favorite haunt off Nahant. It showed itself in the month of July, and remained for at least two whole days, passing between Egg Rock and the Promontory, winding its way into Lynn Harbor, and again, on Sunday morning, heading for South Shores.

The Reverend also commented on another event. On Friday, July 30, 1875, Arthur Lawrence, F. W. Lawrence, and a party of others were aboard the yacht *Princess* off Nahant, Massachusetts, when a large creature appeared nearby, six or eight feet of its turtlelike neck showing for a few seconds, after which the monster submerged. The sea serpent appeared repeatedly, but only for short intervals, and the group aboard the *Princess* decided to capture or kill it. A Ballard rifle was fired at the creature from time to time as the yacht pursued the serpent, getting as close as forty yards away at times. The monster was black, whitish beneath, and the neck was estimated as being about two and a half feet in diameter. A dorsal fin was noted, flippers were believed to be on the creature (but this was partly conjecture), and the eyes were noticed on top of the head. Others who saw the sea serpent at that time were J. P. Thomas and Jack Kelsoe of Swampscott, who were fishing in the vicinity.

When the Reverend Mr. Wood learned of the this incident, he was struck by the apparent attitude of disbelief in the sea serpent in the minds of what he considered too many normal citizens of the Greater Boston community. Tongue in cheek, he wrote the following:

> Some persons on board the yacht *Princess* had the temerity to see, between Nahant and Egg Rock, a marine creature exactly corresponding with those which had been viewed in the same locality twenty-four years back.
> They even had the audacity to watch it for two consecutive hours, and to come so close to it that they could look into its mouth. Worse than all, they actually sketched it, wrote the account of their adventures, and attested the document with their signatures. The original sketch and document are now before me.
> Perhaps the most unpardonable point of all is that the passengers in question are not ignorant and supersti-

tious sailors, but residents, who are widely known and respected.

They are as follows: Mr. Francis W. Lawrence and Mrs. Lawrence; the Rev. Arthur Lawrence, rector of St. Paul's Church, Stockbridge, Massachusetts; and Mrs. Mary Fosdick. Then there are the two sailors, Albion W. Reed and Robert O. Reed.

Four days after the event Mr. Arthur Lawrence drew up the following statement:

Stockbridge, Mass., August 3, 1875

On the 30th of July, 1875, a party of us were on the yacht *Princess,* and while sailing between Swampscott and Egg Rock, we saw a very strange creature. As nearly as we could judge from a distance of about one hundred and fifty yards, its head resembled that of a turtle or snake, *black above and white beneath.* It raised its head from time to time some six or eight feet out of the water, keeping it out from five to ten seconds at a time.

At the back of the neck there was a fin, resembling that of a blackfish, and underneath, some distance below its throat, was a projection which looked as though it might have been the beginning of a pair of fins or flippers, like those of a seal. But as to that, we could not be sure, as the creature never raised itself far enough out of the water to enable us to decide.

Its head seemed to be about two and a half feet in diameter. Of its length we could not judge, as only its head and neck were visible. We followed it for perhaps two hours. It was fired at repeatedly with a Ballard rifle, but without apparent effect, though one ball seemed to strike it. It was seen and watched by the whole party upon the yacht.

The Boston Society of Natural History then promulgated a paper with twenty-four questions for Mr. Lawrence, and the general result of the questions and Mr. Arthur Lawrence's answers follow.

The locality that July 30 of 1875 was Swampscott Bay. It was in the forenoon, and at times the party was within forty yards of the object. A school of blackfish were in the vicinity. The animal moved from time to time at a speed of six knots. Its head resembled that of a frog or turtle, and it was seen for a total of two hours.

The eyes were high on the top of the head. The nostrils were well defined like those of a turtle. Its nose was six to eight feet out of the water. They could not tell the exact size of the neck. Just above the water its neck seemed to broaden out into flippers or fins, but they stayed under water. The tail could not be seen.

The *Princess* chased the animal all around Swampscott Bay and then the creature disappeared in a southeasterly direction.

A Mr. Jack Kelsoe of Swampscott, mentioned above, was fishing nearby. He actually passed within a few hundred yards of the animal while the chase was going on and agrees with all of the statements of Mr. Lawrence.

Mr. Kelsoe was near enough to observe on the dark surface of the sea monster two elongated white marks, about six feet in length, six inches wide, "and having the ends rounded." Mr. J. P. Thomas, another Swampscott fisherman, who also saw the same creature, said that "it came slowly out of the water, like a large mast."

A Captain Garton, the pilot of the steamer *Norman*, stated later in a Bridgetown, New Jersey, paper that on the evening of July 17, 1875, he was off the coast of Plymouth, Massachusetts. He saw the monster apparently chasing a swordfish, although another observer thought that the swordfish was chasing the monster. Garton called the sea monster "a strange snake-like being swimming rapidly toward the vessel. It seemed to be pursuing a large fish, apparently a swordfish."

The Reverend Mr. Wood writes that

the head of the monster was raised at least ten feet above the ocean, but remained stationary only a moment, as it was almost constantly in motion; now diving for a moment, and as suddenly reappearing to the same height. The submarine leviathan was striped black and white, the stripes running lengthwise, from the head to the tail. The throat was pure white, and the head, which was extremely large, was full black, from which, just above a lizard-shaped head, protruded, an inch or more, a pair of deep black eyes, as large as ordinary saucers. The body was round, like a fish-barrel, and the length was more than one hundred feet. The motion was like that of a caterpillar, with this exception: that the head of the snake plunged under the water, whereas the head of the worm merely crooks to the ground.

At about the same time an unidentified writer aboard the *Roman,* which was on a trip from Boston to Philadelphia, stated that a sea serpent was within a quarter of a mile of the ship and was being chased by a swordfish.

When the swordfish first attacked him he reared his head at least ten feet out of the water, and then dove down once more. These actions he kept repeating, so that we had a fine opportunity to scrutinize him. His head was rather flat, and closely resembled that of a turtle. The fin we first observed was on the back, several feet from the head, while small fins protruded on each side.

The body was at least eighty inches in diameter, and presented a shiny surface, covered with large coarse scales. When he moved his head, the water seemed to fairly boil as he rapidly clove his way, so that by far the largest portion of his body must have been under the water. We estimated his length to be at least sixty feet, but the pilot informed us that a few weeks previously he rose alongside the steamer *Roman,* and they reported him to be 120 feet long.

In March 1884 the Reverend Mr. Wood visited Mr. George Wasson, the famed marine painter, who was eager for the preacher to learn of the sea monster Wasson and a companion, Mr. B. L. Fernald, had seen in 1877. Wasson showed Mr. Wood a watercolor drawing of the sea serpent. Mr. Wasson explained how the monster showed itself off Gloucester about noon on July 15, 1877, and was about fifty to sixty feet long. Its speed was five to six knots, and the beast seemed to rise and fall perpendicularly, or "nearly so." The color was brownish black.

"The day was hazy," commented artist Wasson, with a light breeze from the southeast. When we were, as I should judge, about two miles off the mouth of Gloucester harbor, the monster came to the surface about the eighth of a mile to leeward of us. I was looking that way, and saw him appear, but Mr. Fernald did not, the first time. We immediately noticed the surging noise made, and turning, exclaimed, "What ledge was that which broke?"

This is exactly what the sound most resembled,—a heavy ground-swell breaking over a submerged ledge; and the creature itself looked, both in shape and color, more like a ledge covered with kelp than anything else we could think of, though from the extreme roughness of the surface I remember we both spoke of its being somewhat like a gigantic alligator. The skin was not only rough, but the surface was very uneven, and covered with enormous lumps of varying sizes, some being as large as a two-bushel basket.

Near one end was a marked depression, which we took to be the neck. In front of this, the head (?) rose out of the water perhaps half as high as the body, but we saw no eyes, mouth, fins, or the slightest indication of a tail. . . .

From the way the water closed in over it, and the great commotion caused by its disappearing, we judged of its immense bulk, and we also concluded that it went down perpendicularly. It apparently rose in the same way. . . . In concluding I would say that Mr. Fernald has followed the sea for fifteen years, and is perfectly familiar with all the cetaceans that appear on our coast.

The Reverend Mr. Wood, concluding his article in the *Atlantic Monthly,* commented on the frightening away by humans of the sea serpents as they appear from time to time off the New England coast. "Should it again make its appearance," stated Wood, "it ought not to be frightened away by boats, etc. Above all, it ought not to be shot at. If wounded, it would make off to sea, and if killed it would sink, and probably be lost forever. The only weapon which could be of any use would be the harpoon, and the accounts which have already been given show that in several instances it could have been employed with every hope of success."

4

The Sea Serpent and the Whale

For many years during autograph parties I have made little drawings of various marine activities or locations along with my signature in the front of my latest book, and although I have often sketched Boston Light, Minot's Light, the finish of the America's Cup yacht race, and the Gloucester fishing fleet, the favorite of my efforts through the years has been my attempt to draw the picture of the battle between a sea serpent and a whale.

As I finish my drawing of the seemingly impossible encounter, most of those for whom I sketch smile tolerantly, but whether or not they believe wholeheartedly in the story I tell concerning the illustration is a question.

Therefore, here for the first time I give the story in its entirety—the truth of the encounter between the sea serpent and the whale.

On July 8, 1875, the bark *Pauline* was sailing along twenty miles offshore from Cape São Roque, Brazil, when there was a disturbance in the water near the ship. Captain George Drevar and the members of his crew were able to witness the actual fight to the death between a sea serpent and a whale. Later the master of the *Pauline* published the story of the death struggle as he took it from his ship's log.

The weather fine and clear, wind and sea moderate. Observed some black spots on the water, and a whitish pillar, about thirty feet high above them. At the first glance I took all to be breakers as the sea was splashing up fountain-like about them, and the pillar a pinnacle rock, bleached with the sun; but the pillar fell with a splash, and a similar one rose.

They rose and fell alternately in quick succession, and good glasses showed me it was a monstrous sea-serpent coiled twice round a large sperm-whale.

The head and tail parts, each about thirty feet long, were acting as levers, twisting itself and victim round with great velocity. They sank out of sight about every two minutes, coming to the surface still revolving; and the struggles of the whale and two other whales, that were near, frantic with excitement, made the sea in their vicinity like a boiling cauldron; and a loud and confused noise was distinctly heard.

This strange occurrence lasted some fifteen minutes, and finished with the tail portion of the whale being elevated straight into the air, then waving backwards and forwards, and lashing the water furiously in the last death struggle, when the body disappeared from our view, going down head foremost to the bottom, where no doubt it was gorged at the serpent's leisure; and that monster of monsters may have been many months in a state of coma, digesting the huge mouthful.

Then two of the largest sperm-whales that I have ever seen moved slowly thence toward the vessel, their bodies more than usually elevated out of water, and not spouting or making the least noise, but seemingly quite paralysed with fear; indeed, a cold shiver went through my own frame on beholding the last agonizing struggle of the poor whale that had seemed as helpless in the coils of the vicious monster as a small bird in the talons of a hawk.

Allowing for two coils round the whale, I think the serpent was about 160 or 170 feet long, and 7 or 8 feet in girth. It was in color like a conger-eel; and the head, from the mouth being always open, appeared the largest part of its body.

Five days after the captain recorded the above in his journal, the entire crew saw the reappearance of what apparently was the same sea serpent.

When the *Pauline* arrived at its destination of Zanzibar and began unloading the cargo at the British Naval Stores, the sailors naturally talked about the strange duel they had watched off Cape São Roque on July 8.

The Reverend Mr. D. L. Penny, who was chaplain aboard the H.M.S. *London,* became deeply interested, and evidently was of the same curious frame of mind as another man of God, the Reverend Mr. Wood, who also investigated sea serpents.*

*I mentioned the Reverend Mr. Wood in the previous chapter. Possibly the Reverend Mr. Penny had become interested in sea serpents in general when he read back in 1872 that the Reverend Mr. David Twopeny of Stockbridge, Kent, had sighted a sea serpent while on an excursion to Lochourn with a friend and his two daughters. The monster was forty-five feet long and probably had at least five lumps on its back. The date was August 20, 1872. One passenger, Miss Forbes Macrae, was so upset that she was "frightened out of her wits" and insisted on being put ashore at half past two in the morning. She walked home "by herself in the moonlight, thirteen miles over wild mountain tracks," rather than risk seeing the sea serpent again.

The Reverend Mr. Penny questioned as many of the crew of the *Pauline* as would talk with him, after which he wrote a report of what the men saw and how they described the two creatures. He even drew a picture of the incident, guided by the witnesses, but later admitted that the whale should have been placed a little lower in the water, and confessed that he drew it higher in the water so that the delineation would be clearer and would show better the way "in which the animal was attacked."

He sent the entire study to the *Illustrated London News* which published it November 20, 1875.

Incidentally, when the ship's company of the *Pauline* sighted the sea serpent the second time on July 13 at seven in the morning, it was then swimming about eighty miles east of São Roque, "throwing its head and about forty feet of its body in a horizontal position out of water as it passed onwards by the stern of our vessel."

Captain Drevar wondered why the sea serpent was often in the vicinity and decided that the broad band of white paint two feet wide on the *Pauline* might have slightly resembled another sea serpent.

Captain Drevar also recorded that three years before, in the Indian Ocean, a sailing vessel had been dragged over by a sea serpent. He is referring to the 150-ton schooner *Pearl*, which in 1874 was reported to have been capsized by a giant sea monster.

"As I was not sure it was only our free board it was viewing, we had all our axes ready, and were fully determined, should the brute embrace the *Pauline,* to chop away for its backbone with all our might, and the wretch might have found for once in its life that it had caught a Tarter."

Bernard Heuvelmans, in his monumental treatise on sea serpents, states that what Captain Drevar may have seen was a sort of marine boa constrictor of fantastic size. Heuvelmans goes on to state that most people draw a boa constrictor winding with its belly toward its victim, which Heuvelmans says is impossible, for "a reptile cannot bend in that direction," as they always coil laterally as Penny shows in his *Illustrated London News* sketch.

The newspapers reprinted the *Pauline* incident. When Captain Drevar reached Akbar in Burma, he read considerable mail, after which he opened the pages of the London *Daily Telegraph*. Reading the paper, he became very disturbed at the cavalier fashion with which his incident with the sea serpent was discussed and wrote to the *Calcutta Englishman*, particularly surprised at writers who used falsehood to refute his statement. I quote the following exerpt:

> The *Daily Telegraph* says, "The ribs of the ill-fated fish were distinctly heard cracking one after the other, with a report like that of a small cannon; its bellowings ceased, & c. To use the eloquent words of the principal spectator, it 'struck us all aghast with terror.' "
>
> If the writer knew anything of sailors, he would not write such bosh. Fear and terror are not in Jack's composition; and such eloquent words he leaves to such correspondents as described the ever-doubtful "man and dog fight." . . . It is easy for such a paper to make any man, good, great, or interesting, look ridiculous. Little wonder that my relatives write, saying that they would have seen a hundred sea serpents and never reported it; and a lady also wrote that she pitied anyone that was related to anyone that had seen the sea serpent.

Captain George Drevar was not finished, however. Arriving back in Liverpool on January 10, 1877, the master of the *Pauline* reported almost at once to Justice of the Peace T. S. Raffles, a man of great integrity in the city of Liverpool.

Captain Drevar had brought four others of his crew who had witnessed the incident.

All the witnesses told their story. The justice of the peace summarized it effectively in several hundred words and had his secretary write it out carefully. Then, one by one the five men swore to what was written, a condensed and legal form in dry, crisp terms of that period.

Those who signed the document were Captain George Drevar; William Lewarn, Steward; Horatio Thompson, Chief Officer; J. H. Landells, Second Officer; and Owen Baker, Seaman.

Thus we leave the story of an encounter between a sea serpent whose color was "darkish brown above and white below" and a whale, which was seen and attested to by five honest men of the bark *Pauline*.

5

Sea Monsters — 1886 to 1948

The 1886 sea serpent made its first appearance near Cape Ann's Sandy Bay, Massachusetts, which lies between Andrews Point and Straitsmouth Island. Halibut Point is the extreme northern tip of Cape Ann, and Hoop Pole Cove lies between that location and Andrews Point. Gully Point is between Rockport itself and Straitsmouth Island.

On a hot, calm, clear evening of July 1886, Albert W. Tarr, whose camp was near Gully Point, excitedly called across to his neighbors. It was between six and seven, and those in the neighboring cottage hurried outside. Sumner D. York, Charles A. Russell, and Edward C. Battis found that Tarr had been watching the ocean with his marine glasses for some time. Finally he had decided that the strange object that he had been viewing was not a figment of his imagination.

The men hurridly assembled themselves on the edge of the upland bordering the shore and gazed in fascinated wonder as a veritable sea serpent swam slowly by them. The serpent's head was close to the water and was of a dark brown color.

Apparently the monster was seventy or eighty feet long, but they could not see enough of his body to estimate his size accurately. The creature swam almost directly toward them for a space of time, until he passed the group just a little more than a stone's throw away.

Off in the distance were two men in a dory toward which the sea serpent swam. Hoping to alert the men, York and the others shouted across the water, but either the men in the dory did not hear them or paid no attention if they did. It is possible that the sea serpent may have been disturbed by the shouting, as he proceeded to submerge before reaching the dory and was not seen again that day.

On August 12, 1886, Granville Putnam and Calvin Pool sighted the sea serpent from a location near the shore at Andrews Point. Pool, the town clerk at Rockport, heard his son William shout to him from a place near the water, asking him to explain what was out in the ocean immediately offshore. Pool swung his powerful surveying transit out to sea and through his eyepiece saw a gigantic monster of the deep. He called excitedly to Granville B. Putnam, headmaster of the Franklin School of Boston, who was vacationing at a nearby cottage.

"There is something strange out there," Pool called over to Putnam. "I think it is the sea serpent!"

Putnam, who had just finished lunch, noticed the time as one o'clock when he went to get his own sea glasses. Then he mounted the rail of his piazza, which was fifty feet above sea level and twelve yards from shore. Describing the monster, Mr. Putnam wrote:

I saw the strange visitor approaching, passing and departing, and I have no question but that I was looking upon the veritable sea serpent. His movement was not like that of the true serpent, which is always lateral as it must be from the construction of its vertebrae, but a vertical one, reminding me of the blood sucker of my youth. The distance over which I saw it pass was perhaps a mile and a half. The day was exceedingly clear and the sea almost like a polished mirror, so calm was its surface. The head was almost constantly in sight, visible, but not distinctly seen since it was partially obscured by the water which was thrown over it as its muzzle or cranium cut the surface. This foamy water was so noticeable that several exclaimed, "His head is white!"

Back of the head I could distinctly see twelve or fifteen feet of the body which showed a slight vertical motion, while back of that where the movement was greater, the depressions were below the surface and the elevations caused a dozen or more ridges. I attempted to count these, but their movement made it impossible. The centers of these elevations were certainly six or seven feet apart, so that I am sure the whole length of the body could not have been less than 100 feet. The tail, which I was eager to see, did not come into sight.

Putnam was constantly questioned afterward as to just how it looked, and he always answered that it looked like a huge sea serpent and nothing else. He believed that the head was as large as a ten-gallon keg, while the thickest part of the body was fully as large as a flour barrel.

A group of friends who had gathered on his lawn while he was watching the sea serpent agreed with him essentially on what he had observed, entreating him to write down the incident for posterity. Among them were Samuel Babcock of the Bunker Hill School and Professor Stephen Emery of the New England Conservatory. Putnam's article appeared in the Boston *Journal,* after which he was subjected to ridicule from various parts of the country, as many papers had copied the story.

At a nearby cottage that August day when Putnam was observing the sea serpent, another group of people watched the same creature. Miss Virginia Henderson of Philadelphia was visiting her sister's cottage at the tip of Andrews Point and with others made a careful observation of the marine monster. Miss Henderson stated that the creature looked about the size of a barrel and was around eighty feet long. A schooner, the *Annie M. Fears,** was cruising nearby at the time, and Town Clerk Pool, as I have stated, had set up his theodolite on the rocks and aided in the estimation made of the creature's size.

These people, all truthful, intelligent, and well educated, agreed essentially in their stories of the serpent.

Not quite a half century went by, and the sea serpent appeared again. It was on Sunday, January 19, 1936, that the Furnace-Prince liner *Javanese Prince,* one day out from Balboa, was proceeding through the calm waters of the Pacific Ocean in latitude 7°42′N, longitude 82°46′W, in the area off Costa Rica. One of the passengers on deck was Robert Saltonstall Ward, later a resident of North Marshfield, Massachusetts.

There were eight people in the group on deck at the time, which was 10:30 in the morning, and chief engineer Gorton was operating a record player which was grinding out relentlessly a popular air of the day, "The Music Goes Round and Round."

Suddenly, without warning, a sea serpent appeared on the port bow, less than seventy-five yards away, cruising in the

*Of the same schooner family as the *Grace L. Fears,* from which Howard Blackburn fished when he was lost in a snowstorm. He rowed to Newfoundland.

opposite direction. It came out of the water at least four feet and probably more on three occasions. Well proportioned, it was in sight for about three minutes and simply disappeared by sinking under the water. The serpent was dark in color and could have been brown or green. Apparently it resembled the sea serpent of Penobscot Bay mentioned earlier in this book, for when Mr. Ward visited me on February 27, 1954, he said that it was similar to the being mentioned by Joseph Kent of Marshfield, Maine, in 1751. I made a sketch of the Ward sea monster under Mr. Ward's direction, which he later approved as being an accurate representation of the animal which he sighted that day in 1936.

Twelve years went by before the next recorded, documented appearance of the sea serpent, which was on August 26, 1948, at eleven o'clock in the morning off the Isles of Shoals, New Hampshire. It proved to be not more than sixteen nautical miles from the location where the people of Rockport saw the creature in August 1886.

A party of four had left York Harbor, Maine, that morning aboard the twin-screw cabin cruiser *Wava E,* bound for Gloucester Harbor in leisurely fashion. They were Harold F. Robie, his wife, Wava E. Robie, Deering S. Roberts, and his wife, Edna H. Roberts.

Shortly before eleven o'clock that morning the men sighted Duck Island, and then, drawing abeam of Duck Island, had buoy N2 in range and headed for it, intending to do some ground-bottom fishing. All four aboard were intently watching the water. The surface of the sea was almost dead calm, and they had just passed through a gigantic school of mackeral which was at least eight miles across.

When approximately one mile from the nun buoy, in one hundred feet of water, Deering Roberts was on the starboard side of the cruiser with Harold Robie at the wheel.

"Say, why didn't you tell me there was a reef over there?"

shouted Robie, throwing the engine into neutral at once. He pointed off to the westerly.

It certainly looked as though the ocean were breaking over a reef. Roberts glanced again at Chart Number 1206 of the Isles of Shoals, and there was supposedly at least one hundred feet of water all around the immediate vicinity.

"That's no shoal, Harold. I don't know what it could be!"

All hands looked intently at the spot where there was a great commotion on the surface of the sea. Then, all at once, the sea was smooth again. Harold Robie stopped the engines, and the *Wava E.* remained motionless for fifteen or twenty minutes.

All hands carefully scanned the horizon for a new appearance of whatever it was which was invading the region around the Isles of Shoals. It is possible that the monster was on its way to the great school of mackerel.

Suddenly, Mrs. Robie gave a shout. "There it is again! Directly astern!"

Surely enough, the sea monster had reappeared in back of the cabin cruiser. This time three distinct humps or loops of the creature's anatomy showed, and the four people realized that they had joined that relatively rare group of persons who can claim kinship because of the fact that they have actually seen his majesty with the curving, snakelike body. The sea serpent rapidly drew away from the cruiser until it resembled another boat disappearing into the distance. The head of the creature, which was not seen when the sea serpent was near the four watchers, may have appeared as the serpent swam rapidly away, but if it did appear, it was too far away to describe.

On January 31, 1954, I interviewed Mr. and Mrs. Deering Roberts at their Marshfield home. Both were firmly convinced that the creature they saw was about one hundred feet long. Mr. Roberts was very familiar with other types of sea inhabitants. He had seen over one hundred porpoises and assured me it definitely was not a group of porpoises as someone always suggests. He had often fished and would have recognized any one of the common fish of the sea, none of which it could have been. He had also seen the "so-called white whale of the Saint Lawrence and the Saguenay," and it resembled in no way that particular being.

In other words, the creature seen that August day must have been a sea serpent. The knowledge of the presence of a real sea serpent was so overwhelming to the four people aboard the *Wava E* that they were speechless for a long time after the monster vanished.

Mrs. Roberts impressed me when she stated that "we were able to look through the arch of the loop at the water beyond."

"We didn't dare tell anyone about it for a long time," said Mr. Roberts, "because we realized what they would think about us. But it happened and that's all there is to it. All four of us saw a sea serpent on that August day of 1948. It was an awesome spectacle that left us very quiet and thoughtful for some time afterward."

Time magazine of January 12, 1953, tells of the discovery off Madagascar of a seagoing vertebrate fish, the coelacanth, believed to have been extinct for fifty million years. Gradually science is coming into possession of authentic information which allows many good scientists to believe in sea serpents without becoming subjected to ridicule.

There are several hundred other sightings or discoveries of the sea serpent which space prevents us from including, but I list a few of them for possible further study by my readers. They include the discovery in 1885 of a forty-two-foot segment of a sea serpent by the Reverend Mr. Gordon at New River Inlet, Florida; the observations made by two leading British scientists, zoologists Nicholl and Meade-Waldo, at

Parahiba, December 7, 1905; the spinal segments of a sea monster found at Henry Island in November 1914; the sea serpent sighted and fired upon by men aboard the British cruiser *Hilary* on May 22, 1917; the serpent sighted near Saint Paul's Rocks off South America by Thomas Muir in April 1920; the sea serpent written about by R. L. Cassie in 1936 as inhabiting the Loch Achanalt; the strange carcass found at Natal on October 25, 1924; the monster discovered at Salvador in 1928; and the fossilized remains of a sea serpent one hundred feet long found some years ago at Marlboro, New Jersey.

Of course, I am not claiming that all of these sightings or discoveries down through the years have been of real sea serpents. What I am stating is that there are far too many recorded and documented instances of the appearance of his majesty, told and written by intelligent persons for other intelligent persons (including the readers of this chapter), to cast aside all the evidence as imaginative stories or mistaken identifications. If a strange fish such as the coelacanth, which scientists vowed had been dead for millions upon millions of years can suddenly reappear to the amazement and consternation of those same scientists, then it is relatively simple to accept the sea serpent. This usually amiable monster certainly has been doing its best to reappear time and again down through the pages of recorded history from the days of the Burgomaster of Malmo before 1666 to the 1948 discovery off the Isles of Shoals.

We have told of many sea serpents having been seen and of one which was captured. "Is there any sea serpent now on exhibition?" you ask. In the year 1946, R. A. Stirton, director of the University of California's Museum of Paleontology, while excavating in Colombia, found a twenty-five foot skeleton of a sea serpent. In a statement issued by Samuel P. Welles, principal paleontologist, the monster's neck was twelve feet long. He had powerful flippers to swim through the water, breathed air at times, and fed on fish. The skeleton is now in the Museum of Paleontology.

I have presented the written and sworn testimony of men in all walks of life—sailors, fishermen, judges, marshals, schoolteachers, town clerks, and lawyers—all of whom recorded what their eyes had seen.

How many other persons have seen the sea serpent? The number may be hundreds more than is usually believed. Before announcing their discovery to the world these persons must realize that they will probably run the gauntlet of ridicule from their own friends for the rest of their days, and many prefer to keep silent. But times are slowly changing. Within the last few years prominent scientists have announced that sea serpents do actually exist.

These announcements come too late for such men as Colonel Perkins and Granville Putnam. Perkins years afterward admitted that he was one of the "unfortunate individuals" whose fate it had been to see the sea serpent and be subjected to the taunts of disbelievers for the remainder of his days. Putnam also became the subject of ridicule for his presence that day in 1886 when the sea serpent appeared, while countless others down through the centuries have similarly been the objects of criticism.

Therefore, in spite of present scientific belief, it will be many, many years before a person who has seen this rare denizen of the deep will be able to tell his story without at least some of his listeners breaking out into broad, indulgent smiles as the narrator relates his own exciting account of the sighting of his majesty the sea serpent.

6

The Scituate Sea Monster

In the late afternoon of November 15, 1970, an excited member of the Scituate, Massachusetts, police department called me at my Marshfield home with the information that a sea monster had washed ashore at Mann Hill Beach, Scituate. That Sunday a group of members of the Massachusetts Marine Historical League had just finished a long hard field trip to Plymouth and were sipping coffee in the east room of the Snow residence, which looks out on the open sea.

We went at once to the scene of the stranding several miles away and an hour later were involved in research on what was actually a monster from the briny deep.

Within a few hours thousands of sightseers jammed all the roads leading to Mann Hill Beach. When they reached the shore, they were simply overwhelmed by the actuality of being in the presence of a giant creature cast up by the sea.

Rumors that the creature was a real sea serpent spread up and down the beach. By midnight Hatherly Road, the quickest way to the shore, was clogged in a giant traffic jam resembling the days of 1956 when the *Etrusco* came ashore near Scituate Light. Parents, children, students, and many so-called experts gathered to inspect the creature, a few of them taking knives to cut off portions of the flesh, which had an odor of fresh fish.

Indeed, several of the visitors must have been hungry, for it was reported later that they had set up beach fires and were cooking "steaks" from the monster. Holding impromptu spits cut from driftwood, they made quite a sight. The next week one restaurant even advertised that they were serving Sea Serpent Soup as an addition to their regular menu.

The police department was overwhelmed but attempted to function through that first night as an information center. Telephones were ringing far after midnight, one woman anxiously asking about the giant whale which had washed ashore. Sergeant Robert Finnie estimated that at least five hundred calls had come in, one of them from the Loch Ness Monster Investigation team in Scotland!

The following day I received calls from London, Paris, and Antwerp. Television star Bob Kennedy interviewed me from Chicago, and later sources as far away as Lewiston, Idaho, showed their extreme interest.

A careful examination which our group from the Massachusetts Marine Historical League made before, and I repeat, *before* people began pulling and cutting the creature apart,* revealed much that the so-called scientists never could see and never did see. What fascinated me most was one of the fins or flippers which revealed talons having fur between the individual members.

A description of the Scituate sea monster, taken from

*To avoid possible destruction of sea monsters the Arkansas Senate on February 16, 1973, passed a law making it illegal to assault a sea monster or to "molest, kill, trample or harm" one. Such a creature was reported in the Newport, Arkansas, area where sightings of a beast "forty feet long with a spiny-ridged backbone" were made. If there had been such a law in Massachusetts in November 1970, scientists would have been able to make a more thorough and accurate appraisal of the Scituate sea monster.

personal observation, notes, and the statements of several experts who reviewed the remains, indicates that when it came ashore the body measured twenty-nine feet, three inches in length, obviously much shorter than it had been, and was devoid of any type of skin. The talons and the fur were evident in the early stages of Sunday afternoon. Originally the indications were that it had four fins, flippers, or protuberances which measured about six feet from body to tip. There are several people who reported to me that they had counted five fins.

The structure of the body without the skin was extremely well preserved until sightseers began to carve it up. The flesh was fresh and firm and showed the remarkable configuration of the body's frame which made it strong enough to withstand tremendous pressure when the creature sank to profound depths.

The entire appearance of this denizen of the sea bottom suggested a monstrous creature which simply overwhelmed and stunned the average visitor's imagination.

From the completely differing features of the Scituate monster, it cannot fall into that common classification of basking sharks, which has often been used by scientists to explain something that they do not understand.

A scientist called our home, and Mrs. Snow told him what she had seen. Later he was interviewed in detail over the radio and used the exact language Mrs. Snow had used in the telephone interview. He was not able to visit the scene before the creature was ripped apart by overexcited enthusiasts who destroyed forever what we saw on the beach that Sunday afternoon in 1970.

As the days went by the monster was bulldozed under the shale, uncovered again, and then buried for the final time. A scientist decided that it was a basking shark or *Halsydrus maximus.* I do not agree and without question cannot associate a creature whose fins have talons, and between the talons heavy fur growing, with what the scientists call a basking shark.

Meanwhile, all over the world various organizations made conjectures, and controversy arose almost resembling in intensity that which occurred in the year 1848 between Darwin and Owen.

Charles Darwin, famed for his theory of man, and Sir Richard Owen, then curator of the Hunterian Museum in England, almost fought a duel because Owen scoffed at Darwin's statements concerning his belief in the existence of the sea serpent. This fight between scientists lasted more than a generation, and I cannot understand how the outcome of a duel could settle a scientific controversy.

I doubt that the still lasting conflict concerning the creature which washed ashore at Mann Hill Beach will lead to a duel, but if scientists dispute their findings among themselves as I have indicated, they should be a little tolerant of others who express an opinion, even if it differs somewhat from theirs.

I have admired John K. Hammon of the Newbury Street Emmanuel Church of Boston for the following observation which he made, published on December 6, 1970:

> The excitement over the "appearance" at Scituate Beach has somewhat died down over the past several weeks, but please note that there is controversy concerning its identity.
>
> As for me, I positively refuse to believe that the creature washed ashore was not a real sea serpent!
>
> This time I will not accept the findings of the scientists who are just out to "commonize" our world and make it completely prosaic with no room for creative imaginative activity. . . .

Let us prove to the disbelievers that phantasy is still extant and viable in this technological society of ours, that man and mind are more than atoms and germ cells, no matter what is said to the contrary. Basking shark! Hmmmph! Ridiculous!

PART 3

Hurricanes, Tempests, and Blizzards

1

The *Norton* and the *Horton*

Many people have been confused because of the similarity of the names of two schooners, the *Edward H. Norton* and the *Edward A. Horton*. Some of the misunderstanding was caused by the fact that the craft were each seventy-three feet long, were launched within a year of each other at the Essex Shipyard on Cape Ann, and were both fishing vessels. No book now in print has the story of either the *Norton* or the *Horton*.

In this chapter I tell the story of both these schooners, one battered to pieces just a few miles from Marshfield, where I am writing these lines, and the other part of a fine adventure.

As I look out to sea, the Fourth Cliff of Scituate is on the right, the Third Cliff on my left, with the North River running to the sea between them. To the north is the Second Cliff, and beyond is the First Cliff, where the wreck of the *Norton* occurred.

Many still living remember the Portland Gale of 1898, but there was another terrible hurricane which devastated our Atlantic Coast ten years before. A moderate snowstorm had been predicted for November 25, 1888, but in its place, from Portland, Maine, to Cape Cod, came a fierce combination of sleet, freezing rain, and hail, causing tremendously high tides and mighty surf.

There were several spectacular marine rescues that day, many of them led by Captain Joshua James of the Hull Life Saving Station, including survivors from the *Cox and Green,* the *Gertrude Abbott,* the *Bertha Walker,* and the *H. C. Higginson.* *

Shortly after midnight on November 26, 1888, a patrolman from the Fourth Cliff Life Saving Station noticed wreckage, including dories, smashed lumber, and other debris, coming ashore near First Cliff in Scituate. Going down to the rocky beach, the surfman found a dead body floating in, and pulled it high above the reach of the sea. Rushing back to the life saving station, he notified the other lifesavers, and they soon arrived on the shore opposite the wreck of a fishing craft, the seventy-three-foot *Edward H. Norton,* hailing from Wellfleet, Massachusetts.

Out on the vessel, only one man was still alive. He was Martin Allen, a fifty-year-old seaman of 2 Wiggin Street, Boston, a seafarer for thirty-one years. That Sunday morning he had been with his fifteen fellow sailors aboard the fishing craft when the gale hit Massachusetts Bay. By dusk, he explained later, everyone knew they were in for a terrible night. The first mighty sea smashed into the *Norton* at six o'clock that evening, and when it was followed by another and still another, each one as bad as its predecessor, Allen felt that the heavily laden vessel would not survive. After less than ten minutes, a terrific billow completely engulfed the

*Our Snow family in Rockland, Maine, learned of the fate of the *Higginson* in a cryptic telegram from Mate E. C. Road: HIGGINSON ASHORE NANTASKET TOTAL LOSS CAPTAIN TWO MEN LOST.

Norton, and over she went, capsizing with horrifying suddenness in the blackness of that November night.

Allen was pulled down into the forecastle, where he clung desperately to a line. He was smashed back and forth against the bulkheads in the darkness of the overturned fishing craft until half past seven the following morning.

Each wave that crashed into the vessel pushed it closer to the shore. Finally the *Norton* hit the rocky beach at the base of First Cliff across from Scituate Light. By this time Allen despaired of his survival. He thought of his wife and children awaiting his arrival in Boston. Soon the water was neckdeep in the capsized forecastle, and the imprisoned sailor was almost unconscious. But he managed to cling to the line, although his wrists had become numb in the freezing water.

He had no way of telling the time, but the tide could be ascertained more or less by the force of the waves. When it began to go out around three o'clock that morning, Allen noticed that as the billows receded, the lee side of the vessel would begin to rise, for she was in the trough of the sea. This movement was accentuated as the ebb increased. Although terrible seas were still running, Allen thought that he might have a chance to squirm out under the gunwale at the proper time should the roll of the *Norton* become greater.

Still under the hull of the overturned fisherman, he knew that his chance of survival was indeed very small. He would have to free himself of the lines, wait until the exact moment when the hull rolled enough for him to slide under, and move fast enough so that he would not be caught by the next wave or smashed by the hull.

Finally came the wave for which Allen waited. As the water engulfed him to the chin, the seaman cut his lines. Clinging to the bulkhead, he waited for the backlash to strike the *Norton.* The receding wave took the hulk temporarily in tow, and the schooner lifted its shoreward gunwale just high enough for him to squeeze underneath before it settled back on the bottom again.

With a prayer on his lips Allen squirmed out, swam and kicked his way to the surface of the water, and started for shore. The following wave caught him when he was halfway to his goal, swept him in toward the rocky beach and then out again, and smashed him against the hull. This time, however, he was on the outside of the wreck.

Pushing off from the schooner, Allen swam and floated toward shore, getting almost up on the beach when another wave caught him and hurried the sailor in toward land. As the breaker started out again, he grabbed at a rock in desperation and his hand caught on a cleft in the surface of the boulder. There he clung as the wave left him, but he knew that his respite was for only a moment.

Summoning all his waning energy, he tried to gain his feet, but found that he didn't have the strength to stand erect. With the sound of another oncoming breaker behind him, he rolled over and over, each time moving up on higher ground. The billow caught him, raced beyond, and then subsided, but he was near the limit of the wave's surge, and the water left him high and dry.

With victory over the ocean in his grasp, by sheer nerve he then moved himself another ten feet and reached the seawall. There Allen became delirious. Shortly before 7:40 that morning residents of Scituate saw him. Rescuers carried the sailor to the nearby residence of John Conroy. There Conroy and his wife made him as comfortable as possible. He had survived.

At midnight a body from the disaster washed ashore and was picked up on Stage House Beach by the lifesavers. It was later identified as one of the Frenchmen in the crew who had signed on at Prince Edward's Island. At nine o'clock the following morning Captain Frank Curran's remains washed ashore. He was identified by his bushy red hair and beard.

It is believed that Captain Curran had put his fourteen-year-old son Mike in the cabin, and when he later rushed below to save the boy, the two were drowned. The father's body, which evidently had floated free from the cabin, was found hopelessly pinned by timbers, ropes, and nets. He still carried a paper on which was a short prayer to the Holy Virgin.

When they learned of Allen's escape from the vessel, the lifesavers decided to break into the hull with axes. There they found the body of the captain's son and pulled it out through the opening.

On learning the details of Allen's thirteen-hour nightmare in the forecastle of the *Norton,* old-time fishermen of Scituate said that without question his struggles were "the most horrible experience they ever knew a man to live through."

Regarding the storm, veteran lifesaving captain Fred Stanley of the Scituate Fourth Cliff Life Saving Station made the following statement:

It is the worst storm I ever saw, much worse than the one during which Minot's Light went down. That storm, in 1851, came during a high course of tides, while this one arrived on a low course, which makes a big difference in the height of the tide. Look at that meadow!

On a high course of tides the meadows would be overflowed anyway, but this storm on a low course brought a tide four or five feet higher into the harbor.

The story has been erroneously told that Allen was actually rescued through the same hole cut into the hull of the vessel by which the body of the captain's son was extracted, but I have his signed testimony, made after his complete

recovery, describing his miraculous escape. In it he said: "
was washed down into the forecastle, where I clung to a rope
all night. . . . About seven thirty this morning I crawled ou
as a sea ran back, and got to shore. . . . They picked me up
on the wall."

We now leave the shores of Scituate to discuss the adven
ture of the *Horton*.

Down through the years fishing rights of various nation
have been violated by craft from other countries. All of us
are aware, or should be aware, of the monster fishing vessel
from Russia and other iron curtain countries which have
been operating boldly through waters just off the New Eng
land coast, cutting through the nets and lines of United
States fishermen with ruthless lack of concern for the rights
of others.

A century ago, however, it was the Canadian government
which was protesting that the United States was fishing too
close to Canadian shores. Shortly after our own Civil War
the dominion government of Canada began to crack down on
alleged violations of an old treaty concerning fishermen from
Gloucester and the rest of the United States. The treaty
restricted American fishermen from coming closer than
three miles to Canadian shores, and in 1870 the dominion
cutters began to enforce the treaty against unarmed American fishermen.

Early in September 1871, the Gloucester fishing schooner
Edward A. Horton was seized by a Canadian cutter and
taken into Guysborough, Nova Scotia, to await a ruling of
the Canadian court. The schooner's owners, the firm of
MacKenzie, Knowlton & Co, had already lost one vessel,
which had been captured the year before. As their attempts
to find redress in the dominion courts ended in failure, they
decided to make an attempt to locate the *Horton* and if
possible sail her out to sea.

On September 20, 1871, Captain Harvey Knowlton, Jr., a part owner of the vessel, left Gloucester. He arrived on September 27, as unobtrusively as he could, near the mouth of the Alder River, where he established himself at Manchester, Nova Scotia, four miles to the north of Guysborough.

Dressed as a miner, he worked at what he considered a claim until he obtained several samples of ore and went to Canso at the easterly tip of the mainland of Nova Scotia. At Canso, where there was a small colony of American fishermen, he quietly interviewed six men.

Daniel Richards, John Penny, Charles Webber, D. Isaac, Malcolm Macleod, and Peter Gillis all willingly volunteered to help him in his plan to recapture the *Horton.*

On October 3, after briefing the six members of his crew, Captain Knowlton led them through the woods to Guysborough, eighteen miles away. By hiding in the woods whenever any other men were seen, they were able to escape observation.

It was after dark when they reached Guysborough. Leaving his six men hidden in an abandoned barn, Captain Knowlton, still disguised as a miner, went out and made himself familiar with the town, and in particular the wharf where the *Horton* was moored. He studied the channel itself so that he would be ready for action when the time should come.

To his amazement he found that the officials of the Canadian government were so sure that they had the *Horton* safe in the harbor and not in danger of American reprisal that no one had been left on board to guard the ship. After all, her sails, rigging, and much other material had been taken ashore and stored in a nearby loft, and Americans would not have the audacity to attempt such a hopeless venture as recapturing the vessel—or so the Canadians thought.

Back in the barn, the six men were fed daily by the captain, who brought supplies to them once every twenty-four hours.

Finally it was agreed that the night of Sunday, October 8, 1871, was the best time to recapture the vessel. At nine o'clock that evening the stars were brightly shining, and a favorable northwest breeze was blowing. Half an hour later the captain and his men left the barn and boldly walked into Guysborough, six miles away, reaching the center of the town just as the clock in the church steeple sounded the hour of eleven. But the men, noticing that lights were still burning in several of the homes, waited quietly until every last one had been extinguished, at which time they walked toward the wharf.

The fishermen found the sail loft where the *Horton*'s rigging and sails had been kept and took what they thought were the schooner's sails aboard the vessel. Unfortunately the sails did not fit, for they belonged to another craft, and the sailors had to take them back to the loft and obtain the correct ones.

Guysborough Harbor does not have a channel at the wharf, and it was low water. The *Edward A. Horton* was still aground. The tide, however, was coming in rapidly. The men, after bending on her sails and rigging, were ready to go by one o'clock. At this vital moment the suspense was terrible. Any Canadian appearing on the wharf would give the alarm, and, of course, the seven men would be captured.

The minutes went by, with the schooner still on the flats. Finally, shortly after two o'clock, Captain Knowlton decided that the tide was high enough to put out a warp.* In this way the vessel was hove astern so that by 2:30 she was afloat in the channel. With Captain Knowlton at the helm the trim

*To warp a vessel means to move it by putting a line around a piling and then hauling on the line from the vessel.

little craft filled away and showed a clean pair of heels as she passed out of Guysborough Harbor and entered Cheda-buckto Bay.

At daylight the *Horton* was outside of Little Canso, and Captain Knowlton shaped her course south southwest in order to obtain a good offing. A fresh breeze from the north-west helped her far off shore, and her course was set for the Gulf Stream. This southwesterly course was followed until October 11 when the *Horton* ran into a storm, a blow which developed into a severe easterly gale and badly damaged the vessel's foresail.

On the third day out a steamer appeared. Captain Knowl-ton altered his course, and since the steamer did not change hers, she disappeared over the horizon. Knowlton had made up his mind that in case an English cruiser attempted their capture, he would burn the *Horton.*

Continuing a course which took the schooner directly across the southwest part of George's Banks, he then set her bow for Cape Ann.

Meanwhile, back in Guysborough that Monday morning the citizens awoke to find that the *Edward A. Horton* had vanished.

Word soon reached Gloucester that the *Horton* was on the way, but it also said that an English warship was lying in wait a few miles out to sea from Gloucester to intercept and capture the fugitive schooner.

Collector Fitz J. Babson notified Collector Russell of the Boston Custom House that the *Horton* was sailing toward Gloucester and was in danger of capture by a British war-ship. He suggested that an American government vessel be sent to cruise in the same waters. Collector Babson also telegraphed to Portland, asking that the cutter *McCullough* be dispatched to the area. B. H. Smith, district surveyor, then telegraphed to the commandant of the Charlestown Navy

Yard who replied that a vessel would be sent to the assistance of the *Horton.*

During that evening the supply steamer *Fortune,* armed with two howitzers, arrived off Cape Ann from the navy yard, stopping long enough to pick up Robert MacKenzie, one of the owners of the *Horton,* and Captain Robert Tarr, authorized by Collector Babson to take over the *Horton* if they fell in with her. He would assume control in the name of the United States and hold her as a derelict vessel.

After cruising all night and Tuesday morning, the *Fortune* returned to the navy yard and her place was taken by the steamer *Leyden,* which entered Massachusetts Bay on Wednesday, October 11. Two other government craft, the cutter *Mahoning* and the revenue tug *Hamlin,* arrived early Tuesday morning. Both vessels then went to sea in search of the *Horton.* Armed with instructions to prevent any other vessel from interfering with her, they were ready to bring her into port at any hazard.

About this time Collector Babson received a telegram from the collector at Portland stating that the cutter *McCullough* had sailed through Casco Bay and out to sea in search of the *Horton.* Nothing had been seen of either the English warship of the *Edward A. Horton,* whose arrival by this time was eagerly anticipated by almost every person along the New England coast.

At half past seven on Wednesday evening, October 18, the booming of cannon off Rocky Neck announced that the *Edward A. Horton* had been sighted. The news quickly spread all around Cape Ann, and there was general rejoicing. The bells in the church steeples rang, guns were fired, and the people of Gloucester held impromptu parades with drums, horns, pistols, and torchlights in evidence.

Captain Knowlton and his crew came ashore at Rocky Neck, where large crowds soon gathered. Warned of the

possibility of the *Horton*'s coming, newspaper reporters from
as far away as New York were there to record the safe arrival
of the schooner. The Gloucester Cornet Band had been
called out for the occasion. Rendering several stirring patriotic airs on Front Street, the band then marched to Rocky
Neck, escorted by a drum corps and a torchlight procession.
There they went to the residence of Captain Knowlton and
serenaded him for half an hour.

In spite of disagreeable weather, crowds of people followed
the procession. There was general jubilation, shouting, the
firing of guns, and the sending up of rockets on the way,
making it an evening long to be remembered.

Thursday morning arrived and the celebration began
again and continued all that day. The band paraded up and
down the main streets playing patriotic airs. It had been
arranged that at eight o'clock a great meeting would be held
at the town hall, which was crowded to its utmost hours
beforehand. Meeting Chairman Benjamin H. Corliss was the
first speaker. He reviewed the many grievances of American
fishermen, stressing his disgust at the persistent course of
aggravation and aggression maintained by the dominion government.

After another speech by B. H. Smith, Mr. Corliss presented Captain Knowlton and his crew a purse of $1,000 as
a mark of esteem and a "slight testimonial" of the great
service they had rendered the fishing interests in thus daring
to take possession of the *Horton*.

For the next few weeks the people of Gloucester wondered
what the British government would do and how the Canadians would act. Collector Babson applied for another set of
papers on the grounds that the government had no claim
upon any vessel coming into port after having lost her papers.

No violation of law had been committed since the vessel

had been abandoned by the officers who had her in charge and no violence was used in her recapture.

Cape Ann remained in a state of excitement for several weeks afterward as it was rumored that the Canadians would arrive in Gloucester and sail the *Horton* to sea again some dark night. Such precautions were taken that it would have been impossible for anyone to steal the *Horton* and escape with her out of the harbor.

Canada and England, however, exchanged correspondence regarding the seizure of the *Horton*. It was agreed that prize money which the captors had been about to receive should be forfeited on account of the carelessness used in guarding the vessel. The Committee of Council reported that under the circumstances it did not feel called upon to recommend the reclamation of the vessel by the dominion government. It was decided that such dignified conduct as accepting the escape of the *Horton* as a fact would serve to promote friendliness with the United States, which was the "earnest desire of England."

The words of "Yankee Ned," an unidentified Gloucester writer of the period, shall end this chapter.

ESCAPE OF THE *HORTON*

by "Yankee Ned"

Under the canopy of blue,
Under the starlit sky
They crept—the daring, manly crew—
To cut her out, or die!

Into the store they climb,
With darkness all around;

Their nimble fingers quickly find
That every sail is sound.

With hank and halyard stout,
Her wings were bent anew—
Those gallant lads they ran her out
Across the waters blue.

Away from Scotia's shadowy shore,
With cruisers on her lee,
She travels o'er the deep once more,
To Cape Ann's port—she's free!

Old Eastern Point is dead ahead
And the skipper's home in sight,
With flying colors she is sped
Safe into port at night.

The spirit true of 'seventy-six
Lives in the land today:
Thank God!—and no Dominion cliques
Shall bar the Yankee's way.

2

The Gold of the *Central America*

A California miner who had been among the first to find gold on the American River in 1848 finally decided that he had enough money for his future wants. He took a third of a million dollars in gold with him in 1857 when he left the Sacramento area. Traveling to San Francisco, he soon became overwhelmed by the glitter of the great city and fell in love with a young girl of outstanding beauty. In the next few weeks the miner lost all his money.

This successful gold miner had been carried away by the girl's attractiveness and apparent fondness for him. He asked her to marry him, and was delighted when she accepted. Thereupon he entrusted all of his savings to her hands, and then she vanished.

The distraught, unhappy man, frantic with remorse and the realization that the girl had made a fool of him, slowly traced her steps until he heard that she had gone aboard the steamer *Sonora*. He learned the steamer was about to sail for Panama, where the passengers would be transferred to another craft across the isthmus in the Atlantic Ocean.

The miner hurried to the *Sonora* but was too late. When he arrived at the Embarcadero in San Francisco, the *Sonora* was fifty feet out from the dock. In plain view on the upper deck was his intended bride, dressed in newly purchased finery. The *Sonora* gave several sharp, penetrating whistles as she headed for the Golden Gate, and the miner stormed and swore.

Then he shouted for everyone to hear that he was placing a curse on all the gold aboard the ship and announced he was going to jump into the harbor to his death. Uttering his final imprecations at the girl he had planned to marry, he stood at the very edge of the pier and briefly surveyed the scene. Then he leaped down off the wharf, his curses plainly heard by those still on the pier as the water closed over him.

The steamship *Sonora* left San Francisco on August 20, 1857. Arriving in Panama, the money and passengers were taken across the isthmus on Friday, September 1, and transferred to the packet steamer *Central America.*

The *Central America* sailed from Aspinwall City (now known as Colón), Panama, September 3, under Captain W. L. Herndon,* who at forty-four carried the rank of commander in the United States Navy. He had assumed this command two years before and had already taken thousands of men and women to Aspinwall City and brought back no less than $32,800,000 in gold.

Reaching Havana, Cuba, on this voyage, the *Central America* unloaded freight. Then, on September 8, she left for the United States, carrying 101 crew members and 474 passengers.

A gale began that same day, and as the ship proceeded

*His sister was Ellen Herndon, who had married the great naval scientist Commander Matthew Fontaine Maury.

toward New York, the wind increased in intensity. Late Thursday night, September 10, the straining of the ship's hull was evident to everyone aboard, and by Friday morning the creaking and groaning of the vessel had grown worse. Therefore, it was no surprise to Captain Herndon when he was informed that the ship was beginning to leak in the seams amidships, and shortly after this report the water started to pour in by the barrelful. Soon it had filled the entire hold of the ship, in spite of steady pumping, and when it reached the boilers there was a terrible hissing sound as the fires went out one by one. With the fires dead the pumps became useless, and a gigantic bucket brigade was formed. The crew and passengers pitched in with such enthusiasm that they gained on the water for a time and the fires were rekindled.

Unfortunately, elation was short-lived, for the water soon began rising once more, and when the fires went out this time, it was forever. Bailing continued, hour after hour. Entirely at the mercy of wind and waves, the rolling, pitching steam packet soon became waterlogged. The *Central America* was now off stormy Cape Hatteras.

By the morning of Saturday, September 12, it was apparent to almost everyone that the *Central America* was doomed and that the time of her sinking would be only a matter of hours. Still the bailing went on, and the passengers carried out this arduous task without complaint. The storm had now developed into a hurricane with waves twenty and thirty feet high.

At two o'clock on Saturday afternoon all hands were heartened by the lookout, who reported a sail to windward. Within the hour, the Boston brig *Marine* (her master Captain Burt) came alongside and passed under the stern of the wallowing ship.

There were five lifeboats on the *Central America,* two of which were now launched into the sea. They were destroyed at once by the waves. Three boats remained, one of which was in poor condition, having been struck by several heavy seas which had swept across the boat deck.

The next launching, at four o'clock in the afternoon, was successful. The boat then made a series of trips loaded with women and children until all but the men were aboard the *Marine.* By this time there was some distance separating the two craft.

On the next trip the chief engineer and fifteen others started in the lifeboat for the brig. When the final passenger to be rescued by the lifeboat was about to leave, Captain Herndon stepped quickly toward him.

"Please give this watch to my wife," he said. "Tell her from me that I. . . ." Herndon could not finish and walked away. The lifeboat descended into the sea and made the stormy crossing in the gathering darkness to the *Marine.* It never returned to the *Central America.*

Herndon went to the bridge of his ship and watched the remaining passengers as they continued to bail. An hour later the decks were awash and, of course, all bailing stopped. The order came for life preservers to be handed around to the passengers, and Captain Herndon told his officers that although he would never leave the ship, they should do everything they could to save themselves.

Some time later another ship came along, the *El Dorado,* but her master, Captain Stone, misunderstood Captain Herndon and thought the latter had indicated the *Central America* would be able to stay afloat until morning. By waiting, the *El Dorado* could take off the remaining survivors under the better conditions which daylight offered.

As the night wore on Captain Herndon had the foreyard set down. Trying desperately to get the *Central America* before the wind, he found that no canvas was strong enough to endure the gale then blowing. There was nothing else to do but cut away the foremast, out of which a crude sea anchor was built and put astern.

Now the water was approaching the level of the main deck. The sailors bent on fragments of sail, but in vain, for the *Central America* began to roll heavily in the trough of the sea.

Captain Herndon told Chief Officer Van Rennselaer that he was going below. In a short time the captain reappeared on the bridge, attired in full dress uniform. Removing the oilskin cover that kept his naval cap dry, he stood firm and erect—a striking figure.

The ship gave a warning lurch, recovering only with the greatest difficulty. Captain Herndon asked for volunteers to chop free the wheelhouse and make a raft of it.

Suddenly, the vessel gave two more violent lurches, after which she listed to an angle of forty-five degrees. The moment of disaster was now at hand.

With scores struggling on the decks, the ship plunged stern first with "every timber quivering" and disappeared under the mighty waves. After the *Central America* went down, Herndon and several in the crew could be seen floating on the wheelhouse for a time, but soon the others washed off and the captain was alone.

As they drifted away on fragments of the forecastle, members of the crew watched him attempting to keep his balance. Holding his telescope, Herndon waved back to those on the wreckage. His uniformed body was ramrod straight as the wheelhouse took him into the mist and out of sight forever.

One of the most brilliant naval officers of his time, Herndon had distinguished himself in the war with Mexico. Stationed at the Washington Naval Observatory for several years, he later explored the Amazon River under the direction of the United States government.

On the morning after the sinking, September 13, 1857, the Norwegian bark *Ellen* came running down with a free wind and sighted wreckage from the *Central America*. Soon the cries of passengers still afloat rose from the broken timbers. By nine o'clock the *Ellen* had picked up thirty-one survivors after they had spent hours in the sea.

Passengers later told many thrilling narratives of personal sufferings. A Mr. George furnished an idea of the terrors of a night on a storm-tossed ocean. He was one of the hundreds who had supplied themselves with life preservers and pieces of planking and who preferred to await the ship's going down to leaping overboard in anticipation of her fate. When she sank, he was dragged with many others on board some twenty-five feet below the surface.

He "heard no shriek—nothing but the seething rush and hiss of waters that closed above her as she hurried, almost with the speed of an arrow, to her ocean bed." He was sucked in by "the whirlpool caused by her swift descent, to a depth that was seemingly unfathomable," and into a darkness that he had never dreamed of. "Compared with it, the blackest night, without moon or star, was as broad noonday."

Stunned rather than stifled, he came to the surface with his sensations "almost as painful, in reaction" as those endured at the greatest depth to which he sank. When he became conscious, after the lapse of a minute or two, he could distinguish every object around him for a considerable distance. The waves, "as they rose and fell, revealed a sea of human heads." Those unfortunates who had lost their life preservers or planks while under water, were grabbing frantically at other fragments of wreckage as they broke off and floated to the surface.

Finally, Mr. George saw the lights of the *Ellen*. He described his sensations.

I never felt so thankful in all my life, for I never knew before what real gratitude was. I do not know whether or not I cried, but I know that I was astonished to hear my own laughter ringing in my ears. I do not know why I laughed. The verse, "God moves in a mysterious way," kept passing in and out of me—through me rather, as if I had been the pipe of an organ.

I never had the slightest doubt but that I would be saved until the lights passed by, and receded in the distance. Then I began to give myself up for lost indeed. But I slowly drifted towards her, until I could make out her hull and then a mast, and I shouted, and was taken up. When I got on the deck I could not stand. I did not know until then how exhausted I was.

The most remarkable individual experience was that of Fireman Alexander Grant. Though but a young man, this was his fourth shipwreck!

When a boy, he had been wrecked on a Fall River schooner in the Bay of Fundy and barely saved his life. Later he was fireman aboard the ill-fated Collins steamer *Arctic* in 1854, and when she sank he floated away from her on a piece of lumber. He was picked up after several days of suffering by the ship *Cambria.* Then, as fireman on the *Crescent City,* he was rescued after that vessel crashed ashore in the Bahamas.

Now, for the fourth time, he was shipwrecked, and, just as the *Central America* went down, he and nine others clambered on part of the hurricane deck, a fragment of which they had previously cut clear. That night they spent on the deck, praying and watching for another craft. They sighted one, the *Marine,* in the morning, but although they made every possible effort to attract the attention of those aboard, they were not seen.

All day and night they scanned the seas in vain. During Sunday morning eight people perished when they were washed off the raft. Then Monday morning young Grant rescued George W. Dawson from a log and later picked up a second man. The raft floated near a passenger on a fragment of what once had been the captain's stateroom.

On the following day only Grant and Dawson remained on the deck, the others having fallen off. That same afternoon, the third since the sinking, Grant sighted a boat in the distance.

I saw a boat three miles off, but could not tell whether there was anyone in it or not, but thought there was. Jumping into the sea I swam towards the boat with all my might. I discovered a man sitting in the boat, trying to scull the boat towards me.

On reaching the side of the boat, the man, who proved to be a Mr. Tice, helped me in. When secured by Mr. Tice, the lifeboat had been full of water. It had been bailed out by him through the aid of a bucket and tin pan which he had found in it, in addition to three good oars, which remained in the boat after being swamped.

Mr. Tice and I immediately pulled the boat as fast as possible to the hurricane deck, and took Mr. Dawson in. We allowed the boat to drift with the wind to seaward, not being able to help ourselves if we had wished, and not knowing which way to pull.

The three men saw a sail on Sunday, the eighth day after the shipwreck, but she disappeared over the horizon. On the ninth day they sighted the brig *Mary* which eventually rescued them.

The three survivors mentioned above who had been rescued by the brig *Mary* actually had drifted no less than 450 miles in the nine days since the *Central America* foundered. For days afterward, ships searched the area for possible survivors still alive in the water, but none was found.

Now, more than a century later, fantastic stories of how the treasures of gold on the *Central America* were ignored may interest the average reader more than an accounting of how many were saved, although human life should always be considered as more valuable than gold. Of those passengers who ignored all the gold and gold dust aboard the *Central America* and survived, many later told of the strange experiences they went through with hundreds of thousands of dollars all around them. Never before in maritime history had there been such a large amount of money lying untouched in the main saloon of a ship.

While the freight lists totaled well over $1,750,000, many in their staterooms counted their wealth in gold by the tens of thousands. In addition to the two treasure chests in the purser's quarters that made up the regular freight, there was more than $525,000 aboard still in the possession of grizzled miners and cautious veterans of the gold fields. Each had taken his substantial hoard right into his stateroom with him and kept his fortune close by his side at all times. Several of the miners are believed to have had scores of the rare Sacramento ingots whose value today is said to be from $5,000 to $10,000 each!

As the storm raged and grew worse, the importance of the fortune seemed to diminish hourly until on Saturday wealthy men tore off their treasure belts and scattered the gold around the deck of the saloon. In some instances full purses containing thousands of dollars lay untouched. Carpetbags were opened and the shining metal poured out onto the deck with abandon. One of the passengers opened up his bag and dashed $20,000 in gold on the deck, offering it to anyone who wished it. It went untouched.

Thus, when the proud steamer sank to her doom, more than two and a third million dollars in gold went with her. As gold is not affected by immersion in the ocean, it still lies at the bottom of the sea, awaiting some carefully planned diving expedition to bring the treasure to the surface again.

The greatest amount of treasure from sunken ships ever recovered off the shores of North America was $1,250,000 in gold and silver brought to the surface in 1687 by Maine-born Sir William Phips. This vast hoard came from a Spanish galleon which had gone down forty-six years earlier off the coast of Hispaniola.*

Nevertheless, it is entirely within the realm of possibility, because of almost unbelievable strides forward in undersea detection, that a substantially larger treasure may be brought to the surface off the shores of Cape Hatteras from the wreck of the ill-fated steam packet *Central America*. In 1857 this proud vessel sank with $2,345,000 in gold which is still on the bottom of the sea off North Carolina.

Of course, don't forget my admonition that there is always a possibility that other powers may control your most carefully laid plans. Nevertheless, the incentive is still there, and with the several new millionaires who have recovered gold from the bottom in this generation, perhaps a reader of these words will be the next lucky one.

Incidentally, the girl responsible for the miner's curse being placed on the gold transported aboard the *Central America* probably went down with the steamer, as her name was never included in any list of passengers saved from this terrible disaster. Of the ship's company of 575, when the *Central America* sank to her doom off the shores of Cape Hatteras only 131 survived, with the lady of San Francisco losing her life along with 443 others.

*See my *True Tales of Buried Treasure,* pages 1–19.

3

Saint Paul's Island

Saint Paul's Island, ten miles northeast of North Cape on Cape Breton Island, has had a long list of fatal shipwrecks since the beginning of its recorded history around 1825. No one will ever know how many unfortunate ships were lost before that time, but it is probable that scores upon scores of forgotten vessels have been wrecked at Saint Paul's.

Before visiting the island, I talked with seventy-five-year-old John M. Campbell, a former superintendent there. He, his father, and his grandfather had all been superintendents of the island. Each one kept a journal, and their records are filled with exciting stories. But long before the Campbells came to the island of Saint Paul's, its rocky cliffs were synonymous with terror and death. The countless shipwrecks that had taken place there could only be identified by a bit of wreckage or a skeleton or two at the base of an isolated headland.

Although the distance from Saint Paul's to Money Point Light on the northern tip of Cape Breton is less than ten miles, in a storm it might as well be ten thousand. When the frightful surf pushes its way higher and higher up the rocky ledges of Saint Paul's, no one can land on the island and no one can leave it. During a gale, Saint Paul's is as effectively cut off from the rest of the world as if it were on another planet. At the height of winter, when the dreaded ice packs crash against the island, its coastline is even more fearsome.

Although the island is scarcely two and three-quarter miles in length and only a mile in width, the contours of its cliffs, chasm, and outer beaches are so intricate that its shoreline measures eleven miles. Because of the constant surf, there are few days when the base of the cliffs can be explored. Almost every bay or rocky ledge and more than a score of headlands and coves have been the scenes of shipwreck and tragedy.

The four really important locations at Saint Paul's are North (or Northeast) Light, South (or Southwest) Light, Atlantic Cove on the east, and Trinity Cove on the west. Atlantic Cove was the island headquarters for many years. There are two inland lakes, Ethel to the north and Lena to the south. Yellowish brown streams flow from these lakes into both Trinity Cove and Atlantic Cove.

Sea gulls are often found at Saint Paul's, and the great auk, now extinct, once lived on its rocky crags. As large as a goose, with short wings and a white breast, the auk could be identified by a milk-white spot under its right eye. Before the species disappeared, museum collectors offered as much as fifteen hundred dollars for a single bird.

At two locations the island's rocky masses rise to a height of more than four hundred feet. The highest point looks down into Atlantic Cove and forms a geographical triangle with the cove and Lake Lena. Four hundred and eighty-five feet above the sea, this peak is the southern point of the triangle, with the lake the northwest point and Atlantic Cove forming the third apex to the northeast. Once called Beacon

Hill, it is now known as Crocan Mountain. The other high area is on the rocky northern peninsula of the island and looks down across the chasm toward North Point Light, which is on a tiny separate island all its own. You can only reach North Point Light by climbing into a hanging chair, built along the lines of a breeches buoy, and pulling yourself across the chasm on a cable far over the water. It is a great adventure.

The island's two lighthouses are officially listed as lying in the Cabot Strait at the entrance to the Gulf of Saint Lawrence. They have been illuminated since 1837. North Point Light burned down in 1916 but was soon rebuilt, and its beacon now shines steadily from a white octagonal structure forty feet high, 126 feet above the sea. South Point Light is a red cylindrical iron tower twenty-seven feet high, standing 156 feet above the ocean. Its light flashes four times every twelve seconds. Also on Saint Paul's is a fog diaphone at North Point Light; a radio direction finder at Atlantic Cove which at times is operated as a radio beacon; and a marine telegraph, weather, and ice report station at South Point Light.

I visited Saint Paul's to delve into its fascinating history of shipwrecks. Several weird ghost stories made my task an even more interesting one. In collecting the facts, the journals kept by the three Campbells proved invaluable.

The first of the Campbell family to live on the island was John Campbell of Argyll, Scotland, who was appointed by the British government as superintendent of the island. His first task was to direct the building of the main station and the two lighthouses.

Three of John Campbell's children were born deaf and two of these unfortunates died in childhood of tuberculosis. Campbell had two other children, Malcolm and Samuel.

One spring day Malcolm Campbell, John's oldest son, and four men from the island boarded a vessel stranded on the coast and found her to be the schooner *Joseph,* with not a living soul aboard. They brought her back to the cove, where Campbell examined her log book, but found no hint as to what had occurred. Nothing was ever learned of the crew.

On another occasion, John Campbell participated in a rescue following a shipwreck. On April 28, 1865, the Irish emigrant ship *Pallas* sailed from Cork, bound for Quebec. Aboard were 136 passengers and sixteen members of the crew. On May 30 the *Pallas* was approaching the coast of Cape Breton when a heavy fog set in. At eight o'clock the passengers heard the distant sound of a cannon being fired, but the fog was so thick they could not tell from which direction it came, and the *Pallas* continued at a speed of four and a half knots. Two hours later another cannon shot was heard, this time from close east, but it was too late, and the *Pallas* crashed against the granite ledges of Saint Paul's Island.

Superintendent Campbell soon heard shouts and the ringing of a ship's bell. Going to the edge of the cliff with his wife, he tried to peer across the darkness toward the ship, but the fog was too thick. He saw, however, that the waves were dashing forty and fifty feet up against the cliffs. He could do nothing to help the survivors on the wreck, but he remained on the rocks all that night, waving lanterns and shouting encouragement. Finally, the surf went down a little. The island log book notes:

We carried a boat with great difficulty from Atlantic Cove to the rocks. The ship launched one of her own lifeboats but she filled at once and all in her drowned but three men. With my boat I got the three who were clinging to a sunken rock, having with great difficulty launched my own little lifeboat. It was one of the darkest nights I ever beheld, with rain and snowsqualls.

Later the next day Campbell rescued all the remaining passengers and crew members, most of them "quite naked, having lost everything they had in the world." Eighty-two of the passengers and crew had drowned, seventy were rescued by Campbell and his men, including the captain of the ship. The captain of the *Pallas* went to Sydney several days later and hired the schooner *Nazaire* to transport the survivors to Grosse Island. From there they were taken by regular steamer to their destination—Quebec.

Samuel Campbell succeeded his father at the station in 1874, bringing his two-year-old son out to the "rock" in 1876. The boy's name was John M. Campbell, and it was he whom I interviewed in 1950.

John M. Campbell remained on lonely Saint Paul's until 1890, returned again in 1904, and stayed on as superintendent until 1918. The Campbell family, therefore, played a most important part in the affairs at Saint Paul's for eighty-one years.

John M. Campbell prepared a list for me of vessels wrecked at Saint Paul's. They were the *Jessie, Mitchell, Wave, Deodata, Margaret, Marie Casabona, Canadian, Venesian, Viceroy, Anna, Alfred Taylor, Emperor, Glenlevit, Ollivete, Warwick, Barbara, Norwegian, Duncan, Jane, England's Queen, Pallas, Royal Sovereign, Glenroe, Brunette, Thistle, Isabella, Minerva, Enchantress, Vanguard, Briton Elliot, Turrett Bay, Helena, Arcola,* and the *Elliot.* For every known disaster there are two unknown wrecks in the stormy waters beyond the island cliffs.

Mariners learned to fear the rocks of Saint Paul's long before the beginning of recorded history at Cape Breton. There is good reason to believe that at least one Spanish galleon, driven far off its course, crashed to its doom against the granite sides of this natural bastion.

For years fishermen brought up gold doubloons from the sea bottom at the base of one of the cliffs. Their technique was to dip long poles into pitch and with them reach down to the floor of the ocean. Doubloons adhered to the pitch and scores of them were brought to the surface. The fishermen's crude methods were not effective in recovering the heavy bars of gold and silver which were undoubtedly part of the cargo, and most of the treasure from the galleon is without question still in the water at the base of that cliff.

John M. Campbell told me that one of the keepers discovered a *crocan,* or jug, containing five hundred sovereigns in a rocky crevice some distance above the waves. Evidently a shipwrecked sailor had hid his treasure in a safe place and died before it could be removed. The area where the jug was found is still known as Crocan Cove, at the foot of Crocan Mountain.

There are many ghost stories at the island. First, there is the legend of the beautiful woman spirit which has great similarity to the famous Sable Island ghost story I told in my *Mysteries and Adventures along the Atlantic Coast.* Saint Paul's ghost is said to be that of a woman who froze to death after a shipwreck over a century and a half ago. Salvagers who landed on the island the following spring found the frozen bodies but didn't trust each other's honesty and buried the woman with her jewelry. One of her rings held a large, dazzlingly beautiful ruby, and two of the wreckers swore to themselves that they'd return, uncover the grave, and pull the valuable ring from the dead woman's finger.

The wreckers did return—separately but simultaneously! In the fight which followed one murdered the other, took the ruby, and fled the island forever. Sometime later other sailors landed on the island, found the bodies of the woman and the murdered man, buried them, and went their way. But according to John M. Campbell, the ghost of the woman still haunts the vicinity of her grave, appearing in the dark of the moon to demand the return of her ruby.

Another more or less active ghost is that of a woman who

was drowned aboard the *Irishman*. Her body never came ashore, and those who have seen her claim that she wanders the island on the anniversary of the wreck. This particular ghost can be identified by a white luminous shroud, always clearly visible, which floats about her in the darkness. Another member of the spirit population is the ghost of Martin Power, a fisherman who chose to settle on the island. Power's ghost is said still to appear near his old home, and there is today a cove on Saint Paul's which bears his name.

But John M. Campbell told me the most remarkable ghost story I have ever heard—remarkable because of its amazing mixture of realism and mysticism.

When he was a boy, Campbell had often heard the story of the Negro sailor who had been wrecked on the island long before the lights and the main station were built. Details of the story were never written down, but it is known that the man's body was dug up and moved—not once but several times. One time as it was being moved the head of the dead sailor fell off. It was recovered later and reburied elsewhere. According to legend, this unfortunate separation caused the dead man's spirit to grow uneasy, and his decapitated ghost often roamed the island, trying to find his lost head.

When John Campbell first heard this story as a very young boy, he paid little attention to it. But one night as he performed one of his regular chores and went down to the cellar of the house to bring up potatoes, he noticed the Negro's headless form standing near the potato barrel. It frightened him terribly, and he stumbled up the cellar steps and into the kitchen. Ten minutes later he gathered up his courage to go down again. This time he succeeded in getting his potatoes, for the ghost had vanished.

On another occasion the headless ghost again appeared in the cellar to challenge young John, planting itself directly in front of the potatoes. John rushed at the ghost, but it eluded him and vanished. Time and again the creature would appear to the boy in the cellar until he wondered if its head were not buried there.

Finally, one night John Campbell decided to attack the ghost. He felt that he might better die once and for all than be frightened to death gradually. When the ghost next appeared in the cellar, John pretended to ignore it. He went over to the barrel and began filling his pan with potatoes for the evening meal. Out of the corner of his eye he saw the headless form slowly approaching. Then, just as it came close, John twisted about and grabbed it by the waist.

"Now that I had caught him," John Campbell told me later, "I was determined to find out the truth. It was horrible, for when my hands slid over his soft body and reached his neck—why there was no head at all! That panicked me and I must confess that I ran upstairs.

"We all saw the ghost from time to time after that and came to accept him as one of the things at the island that could not be avoided, like the fog and the storms. I bumped into him quite often, but I never had the least desire to grab him again. I left the island in 1890 and came back twelve years later as superintendent, but I didn't see the ghost again. Make no mistake, I saw him that night and when I grabbed him I felt his chest and shoulders and the hollow where his head should have been. Believe me, it was a frightful experience!"

PART 4

Rescued from
the Depths

1

Salvage Then and Now

In the years 1545, 1628, and 1782 three mighty warships sank to the bottom of the ocean under similar conditions, with great loss of life in each case. They were the *Mary Rose* of England, the *Vasa* of Sweden, and the *Royal George* of England.

Although attempts were made to bring up each ship from the bottom at the time of the disaster, none was successful. However, more than three centuries later the Swedish ship *Vasa* was brought to the surface by men with remarkable patience and ingenuity. Long before this time the other two craft had disintegrated, but the *Vasa* proved to be in a fine state of preservation. The reason was that the *Teredo navales,* which destroys wooden ships under water, is unable to survive in the Baltic Sea, where the water is less saline than in the Atlantic Ocean.

The first disaster, that of the *Mary Rose* 429 years ago, is almost completely shrouded in antiquity, but I have been able to gather together the essential facts.

An eyewitness to the sinking, Sir Peter Carewe,* wrote that after the English and the French had fought each other off Spithead, the English Navy came into the harbor. Then the French ships harried the coast, approaching right up to Spithead itself.

When King Henry VIII heard that the French were near Spithead, "he fretted, his teeth stood on an edge, to see the bravery of his enemies, to come so near his nose, and he not able to encounter with them."

The king commanded that all ships sail to Portsmouth to repel a possible invasion. The monarch then left to go aboard the *Greate Henry,* anchored at Spithead.

"The Frenchmen, perceiving that they could do no good by tarrying there, departed again to the seas."

King Henry went out aboard the *Greate Henry* "and was there served by the Lord Admiral, Sir George Carewe, this gentleman, Peter Carewe, and their uncle, Sir Gawen Carewe; and with such others only as were appointed to that voyage and service. The king, being at dinner, willed someone to go up to the top and see whether he could see anything at the seas."

Three or four ships of the French fleet were sighted, and King Henry ordered everyone alerted. The monarch then went ashore.

Shortly afterward Sir George Carewe of the *Mary Rose* went aboard his ship, calling for all hands to take battle stations and ordering the sails hoisted at once. The command was scarcely given when the *Mary Rose* began to go over on her beam end, or cant over on one side. Then she started to fill with water and sink.

*The details are in *Archeologia,* Volume XXVIII. They are taken from a manuscript which in the year 1847 was in the possession of Sir Thomas Phillip, Bart.

"It chanced," wrote Peter Carewe, "unto this gentleman, as the common proverb is 'the more cooks, the worst potage.' " Carewe stated that a hundred able, expert mariners, jealously "contending in envy," refused to help each other and thus perished in confusion. King Henry watched in horror as the great warship slowly sank beneath the waves.

Meanwhile, 105 ships of the British Navy chased the French fleet over the horizon and encountered no resistance. Returning to Spithead, they picked up a handful of survivors from the *Mary Rose,* but it was too late for most of the ship's company.

On July 23, 1545, Lord Russell wrote to Sir William Paget concerning the wreck. In the British State Papers,* Russell speaks of the *Mary Rose,* which "through such reckeness and great negligence should be in such wise cast away."

The next day John Viscount Lisle also wrote to Sir William Paget that "the two hulks, the *Jesus of Lubick* . . . and the *Sampson* . . . are brought unto the *Mary Rose* because they must weigh her up."

On August 7, 1545, the Duke of Suffolk wrote to Paget that the Lord Admiral "had a good hope of the weighing upright of the *Mary Rose* this afternoon or tomorrow."

And so it went through the remainder of 1545, but "this afternoon or tomorrow" never came. The years and then the centuries went by.

A quote from an unknown poet of the period shall end our discussion of the unfortunate *Mary Rose:*

In the deep Bay of St. Helen's O.
There she lay, e'en till this day.

*Volume 1, page 793.

In the spring of the year 1628 the new Swedish warship *Vasa,* then in Stockholm Harbor, was moved to the dock near the royal palace, where the great task of getting her armament and ballast aboard began. Final loading was completed the first week in August.

On Sunday afternoon, August 10, the *Vasa* was warped from the royal palace against a light breeze to start her first real voyage. Suddenly a squall caught her, and the *Vasa* heeled to port, a bad list developing at once. An attempt was made to haul the cannon to windward to counteract the list, but before this could be done the water poured into the open lower cannon ports making this maneuver impossible. At five o'clock that afternoon the *Vasa* sank, carrying a great number of individuals to their death.

Of course, blame was put on the builder, who is said to have constructed the *Vasa* in sturdy fashion but with wrong proportions. An opinion on this could not be obtained from the chief designer of the *Vasa,* Heinrich Hybertsson, because he had passed away the previous year. No one, apparently, knew why the lower cannon ports were not closed in time, and this point was not brought up at the court of inquiry which followed. There were many theories as to why the *Vasa* sank, but this question probably will never be answered.

Three days after the catastrophe which befell the *Vasa,* a British engineer named Ian Bulmer was given permission to bring up the wreck. He offered to salvage the warship with the agreement of "no cure, no pay." Working very hard at the bottom of the sea, he managed to raise her to an even keel; but there operations ended, and he never resumed his efforts.

Many others made similar attempts down through the years, but none had any success until Hans von Treileben began diving on the *Vasa* in 1663. Dressed in a watertight flexible leather suit and working from a diving bell with a six-foot hook, he communicated to a ship on the surface by pulling a rope in the bell. Von Treileben was able to bring cannon up from the *Vasa* in 1664 and 1665, and most of them were recovered. The ship, however, remained at the bottom.

Two hundred and ninety years later, in 1954, Anders Franzen began a systematic search for the *Vasa* and rediscovered her in 110 feet of water almost at the site of the naval dockyard. The Vasa Committee then was formed. They reported a plan for the salvage of the entire craft in which the first step would be to lift the ship from 110 feet of water to a depth of fifty feet below the surface, where the ship would remain until further salvage plans were worked out.

In August 1959 the initial raising of the *Vasa* began. In eighteen stages workmen moved her fifteen hundred feet to a location near Kastellholmen, where she remained at a depth of fifty feet of water. The project was completed by September 1959. In April 1961 a large salvage armada arrived over the wreck, and four pontoons were inflated. Hydraulic jacks then brought the hull close to the surface, and on April 24 the superstructure of the ancient warship broke surface. Powerful salvage pumps were brought right on board the *Vasa* at this time.

By May 4, 1861, the world's oldest identifiable ship was afloat. She was brought into the King Gustaf V dry dock at Beckholmen, where a large raft made of concrete had already been submerged at the bottom of the dock.

Mr. John R. Herbert, dedicated Massachusetts journalist and scholar of maritime activities, has visited the *Vasa* in Stockholm Harbor probably more than any other resident of New England. On several occasions during the last twelve years he has made intensive studies during these visits, and he has been impressed with the progress that has been made on the venerable warship.

Mr. Herbert told me that the *Vasa* is on exhibition a short

distance from downtown Stockholm in a building constructed of aluminum. The site has been especially developed. The immediate area is called Vasavaret, which means
the *Vasa* dry dock, where the cafeteria and the workshop are
located.

Sitting on a floating concrete pontoon, the entire craft is
enclosed in a covered aluminum edifice which allows a prac-
tical use of humidification, which is always turned on.

Emphasis is now being placed on the forecastle and sterncastle of the *Vasa*. An elaborate reconstruction of the stern
is progressing very well. In the aluminum shed, the so-called
Baby Vasa or long boat is exhibited.

When we recall that the *Vasa* sank to the bottom of Stockholm Harbor several years before the Puritans settled Boston, we must admire the men who brought her to the surface
relatively recently.

As the reconstruction advances, a problem has arisen over
the size of the aluminum structure. As the sterncastle grows
outward, the size of the *Vasa* is rapidly threatening the limits
of what was intended to be her permanent home. Another
crisis soon to be faced is, what will happen when the time of
stepping the masts arrives? What is to be done concerning
the height of the masts and the obviously lower height of the
roof?

The daily spraying of water and chemicals is necessary to
preserve the craft through the years, and the humidification
system is another vital part of the plan to preserve the *Vasa*.

"Reconstruction is always going on," Mr. Herbert stated,
"but how far this will continue is a matter still under discussion. Visitors may see the craft from two different balconies
or levels, one about twenty feet higher than the other.

"The lower balcony gives you the waterline picture, while
the upper balcony is arranged so that you are able to look
down on the vessel. Visitors are not allowed to go aboard, for

it is necessary that the spraying of water and chemicals continue all the time."

In 1782, 154 years after the sinking of the *Vasa,* another warship suffered disaster in similar fashion, this time again in England. She was the *Royal George.* As with the *Mary Rose* in 1545, the rapid manner in which she was lost has prevented any really accurate story of the accident from being published.

At the time of the disaster, which drowned many hundreds of men and women, the *Royal George* was the oldest first-rate warship in the British service. She had been built at Woolwich, where her keel was laid in 1751. Pierced for one hundred guns, she afterward had two additional ports; including carronades, she mounted 108 guns. She was rather short and high, but still she was an excellent sailer and made a fine record between the years 1756 and 1782.

Lord Anson, Admiral Boscawen, Lord Rodney, Lord Howe, and many others served as commanders of the *Royal George* in this period. Lawke commanded her in the squadron which defeated the French under Conflans, when the *Superbe,* of seventy guns, was sunk by the cannon of the *Royal George.* She also was responsible for driving ashore the sixty-four-gun man-of-war *Soleil Royale,* which then burned.

Carrying the tallest masts and squarest canvas of any English-built ship in the navy, the *Royal George* returned in 1782 from a long cruise. It was noted that she had more water in her hold than usual, and the water did not decrease after she came into the harbor. An order was issued on Saturday, August 14, 1782, for her to go into dock.

A strict survey by the carpenter and others was made before she entered dry dock, and they found a leak not more than two feet below the watermark. Therefore, it was resolved, in order to save time, that she should be laid down at Spithead and heeled over for repairs. Meanwhile, the carpenter found that the pipe which occasionally was used to admit water to cleanse and sweeten the ship was out of order and had to be replaced.

Thus the problem became complicated as the *Royal George* now had to be heeled over at a greater angle than planned so that the water pipe would be exposed for repairs. Most of the guns were moved across the decks from one side to the other, and the actual heeling began.

Suddenly, as the *Royal George* slowly eased over, the officers noticed that she did not stop careening and continued listing until her cant was ten degrees more than planned. Too late it was discovered that the crew had forgotten to seal the scuppers on the lower decks and water was simply pouring into the ship. At that very moment most of the crew were at dinner, but the carpenters and caulkers were still at their work.

Almost finished with the repairs, the men were about to lay down their tools when, without warning, a squall hit the *Royal George* on the raised side, and the listing began again. Discovering the ship's dangerous situation, the officers ordered the signal "to arms" beaten so that they could right the ship, but their efforts were in vain. Eight minutes later she fell flat on one side and rapidly filled with water. The guns, shot, and other heavy material slid from one side to the other and accelerated her descent. She went to the bottom so rapidly that the confused officers made no signal of distress. Indeed, no one could have helped them if they had, for after her lower ports were under water, nothing could have prevented her from going to the bottom.

At this fatal moment there were nearly twelve hundred persons on board, including about 250 women and children, relatives of the seamen. The families had been permitted to visit the ship and were allowed to remain on board until the order arrived for her sailing. Most of the watch on deck, amounting to about 230 sailors, were saved by the boats which the ships lying nearby had manned and sent to the distress area. Rescue work had to be delayed until the whirl-pool caused by the sudden sinking of the vessel subsided. Then the boats picked up seventy more survivors who came up to the surface after the ship had disappeared.

Among the officers rescued from the brink of eternity was Lieutenant Durham, officer of the watch on deck when the vessel started going down. He had just time to throw off his coat and scramble onto a beam from which he was soon washed. A moment later he found himself floating about among men and hammocks. A drowning marine caught him by the waistcoat and clutched him in such a deathlike grasp that he was drawn under water three different times. In vain he reasoned with the man who still clung to him desperately. Finally, unbuttoning his waistcoat and twisting his shoulders, he slid out from both the garment and the grasp of the dying marine, who sank at once.

Lieutenant Durham then climbed to the top rigging, which was still above the surface. Declining help when a lifeboat came by, he told the rescuers to save Captain Wag-horne, who was in immediate danger of drowning. After the captain had been saved, Durham was taken up and conveyed safely to the shore.

Mr. Henry Bishop, a young man of about nineteen, was saved in an extraordinary manner. On the lower deck at the time of the fatal accident, Bishop was driven by the seas right up the hatchway. At this very moment one of the cannon fell from the middle deck, striking him on his left hand. Never-theless, a few seconds later, he found himself floating on the surface of the water and before long was taken up by one of the boats. Later he found that the cannon had broken three of his fingers.

Nearly nine hundred persons lost their lives in the disaster.

Among them was Admiral Kempenfelt, whose career in the navy had been a glorious one. His flag had been flying in 1781 on board the *Royal George,* then part of Lord Howe's fleet.

Besides the admiral, who was in his cabin writing when the sudden disaster occurred, everyone who was between decks perished with the warship. Captain Waghorne, the admiral's first captain, was fortunately on deck, but his son, a lieutenant on board, was lost.

A multitude of gallant men were drowned. There they were, anchored off their own coast, in fair weather and in smooth water, when in a fraction of a second they were overwhelmed by the ocean which hungrily engulfed entire families forever.

A great number of those who struggled to the surface were saved by climbing out on the topsail yards, which remained above water long after the ship hit bottom. Every effort was made by the boats of other craft in the fleet to save the crew, and they were able to pick up Captain Waghorne, a few officers, and about three hundred people. As the vessel was lying at Spithead, it happened that scores of the seaman and some of the officers had gone ashore. On the other hand, a great many women and children had come on board.

A large sum of money was raised by subscription for the relief of the widows, children, and relatives of those who perished by this fatal accident.

The masts of the *Royal George* remained standing for a considerable time afterward. As the years went by, part of the hull became exposed at low water, but a few decades after the terrible disaster, the wreck sank into the sand and was no longer visible.

On September 9, 1782, a court-martial concerning the disaster was held at Portsmouth on board the *Warspite.* After an examination of such imperfect evidence as could be obtained, Captain Waghorne was honorably acquitted.

I now quote from the pen of a survivor of the disaster:

The water-cock ought to have been put to rights before the shot was put on board. It is my opinion, that had the lieutenant of the watch given orders, to "right ship," when the carpenter first spoke to him, nothing amiss would have happened, as three or four men at each tackle of the starboard guns would very soon have bowsed the guns all out, and by so doing have righted the ship.

At the time this happened, the vessel was anchored by two anchors from the head. The wind was from the northwest, only a trifling breeze; and there was now, a sudden gust of wind which made her heel just before she sank; it was, I felt convinced, the weight of metal and water which rushed in at the port-holes, that sank her, and not the effects of the wind upon her. She had not even a stitch of canvas to keep her head steady as she lay at anchor; she had six months' provisions on board, and many tons of shot.

During the spring following the disaster, a monument was erected in the churchyard at Portsea to the memory of unfortunate Admiral Kempenfelt and his fellow sufferers.

Excerpts from the inscription, which was engraved in gold, follow:

Drop a tear for thy country's loss
On the twenty-ninth day of August, 1782
His Majesty's Ship, the Royal George,
Being on the heel at Spithead,
Overset and sunk; by which fatal accident
About nine hundred persons
Were instantly launched into eternity.

The water pipe, the cause of all this fearful loss of life, is preserved in Portsmouth Dockyard, a memorial of a disaster caused by neglect and carelessness.

It can be said without fear of contradiction that diving and salvage work as we know it today really began at Spithead on the wreck of the *Royal George*. The hull had hit bottom sixty-five feet down, but the top of her masts still were above the surface. The Admiralty attempted to raise her, setting up a cradle of cables between two ships, but this maneuver failed completely. As late as 1799 her mainmasts showed stiff and erect above the water at Spithead.

Many British scientists were interested in bringing the guns and cannon of the *Royal George* to the surface. A diving bell was built, and on the twenty-first of November, 1782, sixteen guns and much cordage were raised. Shortly afterward, by the ingenuity of a salvage group using a newly developed diving bell, the men could work under water for several hours together, and they entertained hopes of being able to weigh the vessel, but all their attempts proved unsuccessful.

Gunpowder was placed aboard and exploded, but divers attempting to recover material had only partial success. Finally, in 1839 Colonel Charles Pasley, of the Army's Royal Sappers,* arrived on the scene with a diving bell. He brought along four officers, twenty-three sappers, and nine men, all soldiers. The diving bell plan failed completely. Pasley now experimented with diving suits. Two failed, but the third, an invention of Augustus Siebe, was successful.

We jump ahead to the year 1840, fifty-seven years after the disaster. The *Royal George* had been taken over by the elements, which reduced the wreck to a mere hulk. Many of the guns had broken through the sides and were embedded in silt

*Military engineers.

and mud, and Colonel Pasley thought that exploding several barrels of gunpowder against the hull of the ship would reveal the cannon once again. Some objects brought up at the time included a dog collar inscribed "Thomas Little, HMS *Victory* 1781," a musket, and a human skull. No cannon were recovered, however.

At this time Lance Corporal Richard P. Jones was probably the best-equipped diver ever to go down on the wreck of the *Royal George*. One day when visibility was practically zero he encountered a smooth object half afloat off the deck. He felt a type of grating and suddenly realized that he was counting the vertebrae of a drowned human body. It was a terrible experience and it was some time before Jones made another descent.

Diving continued off and one for the next few years, but nothing else of importance ever transpired.

2

The *Squalus*

Hundreds and hundreds of ships have been wrecked along and off our Atlantic Coast. Thousands of lives have been lost and countless survivors rescued. In 1925 a new type of sea disaster took place—the loss of men aboard a submarine.

I have always had great admiration and respect for deep-sea divers and sailors who choose to spend their lives on submarines, and, together with the rest of the nation in 1925, I experienced a feeling of almost personal loss when I heard that the *S-51* had been struck and sunk by the *City of Rome* off Block Island. Three men jumped to safety before the submarine sank to the bottom, but all the others were lost.

Again, in December 1927, the submarine *S-4* collided with the destroyer *Paulding* off Cape Cod, and every one of the forty men aboard was suffocated at the bottom of the sea.

The loss of the *S-51* and the *S-4* had proved the need for some method of submarine rescue. Navy Commander Charles B. Momsen was put to work on his new diving lung and began training men to descend more than two hundred feet under water. Commander Allen R. McCann invented a rescue chamber which would go far under the surface of the sea and clamp against the escape hatch of a submarine. Thus the Navy was doing what it could to prevent the loss of lives in the future.

Both these men would assist in the unique rescue of the crew of the *Squalus,* a submarine doomed to be lost less than two weeks after its completion.

On the morning of May 23, 1939, the submarine *Squalus* left Portsmouth on a routine trip around the Isles of Shoals with a crew of fifty-nine officers and men aboard. She had already made eighteen successful dives since her completion on May 12, 1939. At 7:40 that morning the *Squalus* submerged. Nothing unusual happened at first, but suddenly the ship listed, swerved sharply, and threw the crew against the bulkheads. The lights soon went off. Water had entered the vessel through the main engine induction valve, flooding the four compartments of the ship abaft the after control room bulkhead. The *Squalus* went down stern first in 240 feet of water.

Lieutenant Oliver F. Naquin, commander of the *Squalus,* felt the soft thud as the vessel hit bottom and realized that the after compartment must have been flooded. He knew that the twenty-six men in the stern of the ship were drowning and that there was no way of rescuing them. He assembled the remaining thirty-two members of the crew and told them, "You all know by now that we're on the bottom. The after compartments are flooded, but we can go forward. We must wait until help reaches us. We'll send our smoke rockets up every hour or so, and they're bound to sight them sooner or later. We've already released the marker buoy so they'll find us without trouble. We'll be able to talk with the surface just as soon as a rescue ship comes along. That's the situation. All right, Gunner, let's have a red rocket sent up."

Gunner's Mate Eugene D. Craven released a red rocket,

and every man aboard thought of what must be happening on the surface. The rocket would leap out of the water, eject a red cloud, and possibly a fisherman in the vicinity would notice the red flare.

The captain went on talking. "We're far too crowded here. To spread us out a little, I want Mr. Preble to take some of you men forward and then all of you lie down and take it easy. Don't get up for any reason at all."

Mr. Preble, the naval architect who had designed the *Squalus,* went forward with several of the men and every one aboard the submarine lay down on the deck. The hours passed. The men tried to picture what was happening along the New England coast. In Portsmouth, as soon as the signal was overdue from the *Squalus,* Admiral Cyrus W. Cole would start things humming. The men could imagine Admiral Cole sending word to the submarine *Sculpin* to search for the missing *Squalus,* and they wondered how long it would take before their location was discovered.

At 12:40 that day the *Sculpin* was maneuvering in the vicinity and saw a red smoke bomb from the *Squalus.* Five hours had elapsed since the sinking, and this was the seventh rocket sent up. The *Sculpin* soon found the marker buoy. Suddenly, the men aboard the *Squalus* heard the scraping of a boat hook on the marker buoy and then the noise of the buoy being hauled across the deck of a ship on the surface. Though their hearts beat fast with hope and expectation, they remained stretched out on the deck according to their orders and waited tensely for the sound of a human voice from the surface.

Finally, at 1:20 they heard Lieutenant Commander Warren Wilkin of the *Sculpin* speaking: "What is the trouble?"

After Radio Operator John Nichols had explained exactly what had happened, Lieutenant Oliver Naquin stepped over and took the phone; "Hello, Wilkie."

The answer from the *Sculpin* came back at once: "Hello, Oliver."

Suddenly there was a buzzing sound and then complete silence. The mooring buoy had torn loose from the submarine. For a moment or two the *Squalus* had been in communication with the surface—and now—no one could guess how long it would be. The men smiled at each other and pretended there was no need to worry, but the sudden silence had lowered their spirits considerably.

The entire United States Navy had been alerted, however, and in Washington, New London, and Boston, rescue operations were being planned.

Speeding toward Portsmouth over a highway that had been cleared by the police all the way up the coast were three carloads of expert Navy divers. High overhead a twin-engined amphibian brought Lieutenant Commander Momsen, co-inventor of the Momsen diving lung, to the scene of the disaster. For more than twelve years Momsen had been planning for just such an emergency—one requiring deep-sea divers to work more than two hundred feet below the surface.

The *Falcon*, the sturdy rescue ship that had done her duty so well in 1925 when the *S-51* sank after her collision and in 1927 when the *S-4* went down, was making her way up the coast. By midnight the 1–4–3 flashes of Minot's Light could be seen as the *Falcon* kept a steady course for the Isles of Shoals Light.

In the submarine at the bottom of the sea, men became dizzy and sick as the air grew worse and worse. They had been ordered not to change their positions for any reason at all, and as time went on their thoughts grew more desperate. They did not know that two vessels were above them, the *Wandank* and the *Penocook*. Then, exactly twenty-one minutes after five that afternoon, the piercing sharpness of an oscillator bit through their thoughts. Slowly but surely it spelled out the words in Morse code:

WILL INFORM YOU ALL ACTIVITIES MAKE FOUR TAPS IF YOU RECEIVE ME

The men on the *Squalus* knew for certain that help was on the way. One of them swung a heavy sledge against the side of the submarine four times. Then came the biting sound of the oscillator as it spelled out the answering message:

CAN HEAR HAMMER VERY WEAK NOW SEND EACH REPLY THREE TIMES

The hours passed slowly. At 8 o'clock, after no message had been received for two hours, Commander Naquin sent up the following by sledgehammer:

HAVE YOU LOCATED US

There was no reply at all.

Finally, at almost nine o'clock, the oscillator came stinging through the atmosphere again:

WHAT ARE CONDITIONS BELOW

The men swung the heavy sledge again and again, spelling out the message:

SATISFACTORY BUT COLD

The intense cold was slowly sapping away the energy and strength of the men at the bottom. The temperature was only forty-five degrees above zero in the submarine, and it seemed to be getting colder all the time. A little later came the news:

FALCON DUE AT ABOUT THREE IN THE MORNING BE-
LIEVE WE HAVE GRAPNEL ATTACHED WHERE IS YOUR
PERSONNEL

The *Squalus'* reply told the graphic news that only thirty-
three men were alive:

FIFTEEN IN TORPEDO AND EIGHTEEN IN CONTROL
ROOM

And then, as dawn was breaking over the Isles of Shoals
Light, several of the men at the bottom of the sea became
acutely sick. This was only the beginning of a state which
would eventually lead to unconsciousness, but it was enough
to worry their commander. He wondered how long it would
be before the first man collapsed completely.

The *Falcon* arrived at 4:30 that morning and by eight
o'clock was ready to begin operations. At exactly sixteen
minutes past ten the men trapped below heard the welcome
message that a diver was descending to attach a downhaul
wire on which to operate the rescue chamber between the
Falcon and the *Squalus*.

The man chosen for this important mission was thirty-
year-old Martin Sibitsky, at six feet four the Navy's tallest
diver. Over the side he went and down, down, through the
clear, cold water. At two hundred feet there was a slight
delay when the line was snarled. It was quickly freed, and
thirty seconds afterward Sibitsky's feet hit something solid
and gray. It was the submarine *Squalus*.

"I'm on the submarine!" he cried into the phone.

Commander Momsen himself was in charge. "That's
fine," he replied. "Take your time." Momsen knew that at
240 feet below the surface of the sea a man's intelligence and
strength are those of a three-year-old child. The pressure of
the water is too great for clear thinking or quick acting.

Ten minutes later Sibitsky reported, "I see a deck plate marked *windlass.*"

Twenty minutes afterward his next message came through. "I've landed inboard of the port rail and forward of the mast. I am now six feet from the escape hatch cover. Okay to send the downhaul wire to me now."

When the men below on the submarine heard the sound of Sibitsky's feet on the deck, they were nearly frantic with joy. But through their excitement Naquin's voice came to them, calm and unemotional; he stood close to them in the darkness and spoke in a low tone, "Take it easy men—it may be a long time yet."

Meanwhile Sibitsky secured the downhaul wire to the submarine and returned to the surface.

Two of the chosen divers, John Mihalowski and Walter Harman, entered the rescue chamber. Inventor McCann was ready to direct them from the deck of the *Falcon.* The McCann rescue chamber is shaped like a huge inverted pear, eight feet across and about twelve feet high. Air pressure fed from the ship on the surface keeps the water from rising inside the chamber, which is usually open at the bottom.

McCann signaled for the boom to hoist his invention from the deck of the *Falcon* into the water, and a short time later the rescue chamber was bobbing up and down beside the *Falcon.* The two men inside the chamber were unable to stand because of the valves and guages which almost filled the top part of the chamber. They adjusted the buoyancy for the descent to the *Squalus* and then awaited orders to start the motor which would operate the cable running from the surface to the bottom.

"Blow all ballast in the lower compartment," McCann called over the telephone to the two men inside the chamber.

"All ballast is blown," the men replied.

Now the divers reduced the air pressure so that the water

came flooding in. Then they started the motor exhaust valve; the downhaul reel began to revolve, and the rescue chamber began its descent. Minutes passed as the diving bell moved slowly downward. Finally the gray hull of the submarine *Squalus* loomed into view, and the rescue chamber settled comfortably around the submarine's outer hatch cover. The divers soon bolted the escape chamber to the cover.

The next few moments are memorable in submarine history. Ankle deep in water at the bottom of the escape hatch, Mihalowski began to swing the wheel of the submarine's deck hatch. The hatch soon loosened, and he threw it open with a quick push. Letting himself down into the lower hatch, Mihalowski made his way carefully until he had found the handhold. Then, standing on the lower hatchway, he tapped the cover smartly with a wrench and swung the cover open.

Below in the torpedo room was a circle of joyous faces smiling up at him, and he, too, began to grin.

"Hi, fellows," he said. "Here we are."

They were simple, everyday words, but they meant life and hope to the men of the *Squalus.*

Seven survivors were chosen to go on the first trip to the surface. Lieutenant Naquin selected them carefully. One officer was needed, and the civilian, Preble, of course, should go with the group. Five enlisted men were chosen to make up the complement, and the seven selected soon climbed the ladder into the rescue chamber, inhaling the fresh air as they went. Once in the chamber, the men sat down on the wide rim above the compartment hatch. Then at thirteen minutes past one they were ready for the ascent.

Harman had already begun feeding fresh air into the torpedo room. "We'll be back," he assured those remaining in the submarine.

After what seemed like several hours, but was actually

only nineteen minutes, the diving bell broke through the water at the surface. A great shout went up from the men on the *Falcon*. The order came over the telephone from Commander McCann, "Inside the chamber, open the hatch."

The hatch flew up, and Lieutenant Nichols, the officer chosen for the first ascent, looked out. He was helped to the deck of the *Falcon* and escorted to the sick bay. Then the other six survivors were taken off and followed Lieutenant Nichols to obtain medical treatment.

An epic of the sea had taken place—the first persons in history had been saved from a sunken submarine by a diving chamber.

The next two trips went successfully, but as the rescue chamber made its final ascent with the last eight survivors, the lines stuck at 160 feet. Four divers were sent down to free the lines, but they all failed in their efforts. Hour after hour went by and darkness came. Finally it was decided to attempt the desperate task of handworking the chamber to the surface. The time was midnight when the order came to blow just enough ballast inside the diving chamber to neutralize the pressure from outside.

Slowly the rescuers blew the ballast from the diving bell, and then four divers began to pull the chamber along the wire cable by hand. Every few feet they had to pause while the pressure was adjusted. If they pulled too fast, the chamber might shoot to the surface out of control, crushing the divers and possibly killing the men inside.

The desperate attempt succeeded. Half an hour later, the escape chamber was on the surface alongside the *Falcon*. All thirty-three of the *Squalus* survivors were safe aboard the *Falcon* after one of the most thrilling rescues of all times.

Eventually the *Squalus* was raised. The cost of refitting her was $1,450,000, and she was put back into service with the new name *Sailfish*.

One mystery concerning the *Squalus* has never been properly explained. The body of one man, supposedly drowned on the submarine, was never discovered. This mystery will remain forever.

In World War II the submarine *Sculpin,* which had stood by the *Squalus* when the latter went down near the Isles of Shoals in 1939, was put out of action by an enemy destroyer, which took forty-two prisoners from the *Sculpin.* On December 31, 1943, twenty-one of the *Sculpin* survivors were being taken to Truk aboard the Japanese carrier *Chuvo.*

The *Chuvo* was torpedoed by the *Sailfish,* the former *Squalus,* and only one American escaped—a tragic, coincidental happening.

3

From the *Turtle*
to the *Scorpion*

Full fathom five the father lies.
  Of his bones are coral made;
Those are pearls that were his eyes;
  Nothing of him that doth fade
But doth suffer a sea change
Into something rich and strange.
Sea-nymphs hourly ring his knell.
  Ding-dong!
Hark! now I hear them—Ding-dong, bell!

So did William Shakespeare give us Ariel's song more than three centuries ago, but that song, sadly enough, is just as appropriate today.

On many occasions and in several books and articles I have discussed the loss of the five American submarines which have gone to their doom off the New England Coast. They are the *O-9*, the *S-51*, the *S-4*, the *Squalus*, and the

Thresher. Having related the sagas of all these submersibles in various books which I have written, I have come to the conclusion that the submarine service of the United States is one of the most hazardous of any of our armed forces.

Although ships have sailed and fought on the seven seas for thousands of years, the first submarine in combat was the *Turtle* in the American Revolution. The tale of the *Turtle* is not known to the average reader. I recall one day in 1946 when for the first time I told the story over the radio. We had journeyed from Boston to Saybrook, Connecticut, the home of David Bushnell, to give an on-the-scene broadcast of the tale of America's first submarine over the Yankee Network's WNAC.

I related how David Bushnell of Saybrook built a submersible named *Turtle* which was used in New York Harbor in an attempt to sink Admiral Howe's flagship, the *Eagle,* in the year 1776. On September 6 the *Turtle,* piloted by Sergeant Ezra Lee, was maneuvered by three canoes to a point off Whitehall Stairs in Manhattan. Sealed inside the one-man submarine, Lee could operate a vertical propeller by a left-hand pedal and a forward propellor by a right-hand pedal, while looking through a peephole and breathing through two snorkels which reached to the surface for air. When the *Turtle* was in place he could work an augur handle to bore into an enemy craft's hull to place a bomb.

On the surface of the water Lee piloted the *Turtle* toward the *Eagle* until his craft hit the side of the flagship with a gentle bump. Then he submerged. A sailor on deck noticed the craft but thought it was an old waterlogged barrel. Actually the *Turtle* was egg-shaped.

Unfortunately for Lee, the *Eagle* was heavily sheathed in copper, and although he bored and bored with great diligence, he could not penetrate the metal. He finally gave up in despair. Coming to the surface, the *Turtle* was detected by several British redcoats in nearby boats. When they started across to find out what was going on, Lee released his underwater bombs, which went off with a great explosion.

No one was injured, but the redcoats were frightened and rowed away from the scene. The Americans ashore launched several whaleboats and reached the *Turtle*. They released the hatch, for Lee was sealed inside, and pulled America's first submarine pilot out. By this time the sergeant was unconscious, although he soon recovered.

The *Turtle* then swamped and went to the bottom. After some time it was salvaged and taken to Virginia, where it attacked ships of the British fleet there.

Later on, George Washington praised the efforts of inventor David Bushnell and Sergeant Ezra Lee, saying that the *Turtle* was an "effort of genius."

In Civil War days a Confederate underwater craft, the *Hunley,* sank the U.S.S. *Housatonic* in Charleston Harbor. The two events of the *Turtle* and the *Hunley* constituted our actual submarine encounters until World War I.

The submarine as an offensive weapon played its first important role in World War I and expanded severalfold in World War II. Indeed, we should all salute the submariners who were *"loyal jusqu'à la mort"* in their final patrols. The enigmas and mysteries of those final fatal patrols are many, but until the deep gives up its dead, just what happened in scores of utter vanishings of these underwater craft of the United States will remain a mystery.

In World War I the Germans lost 178 out of 272 submarines, and in World War II over 700 U-boats were lost. The Japanese in World War II lost 128 submarines, and at the end of the war had only 58 submarines, many of them nonoperational.

As Fleet Admiral Chester Nimitz said before his own death, "We who survived World War II salute those gallant officers and men of our submarines who lost their lives. We shall never forget that it was our own submarines that held the lines against the enemy."

During World War II American losses in this branch of the service were a total of fifty-two submarines, 374 officers and 3,131 men. This represented 18 percent of the officers and 13 percent of enlisted personnel who saw combat duty. Although the figures may seem high at first glance, when compared to enemy losses they were actually lower.

Just as during the Revolution George Washington had praised the efforts of Bushnell and Lee, at the time of the *Thresher* disaster in 1963 President John Kennedy eulogized the men of the lost submarine, stating that "these brave men have joined their comrades who have died in battle."

On April 10, 1963, the Navy announced that the *Thresher* was "overdue and presumed missing." She had been conducting deep diving tests about 220 miles away from Boston and had 129 persons aboard. Located later 270 miles east of Boston, the *Thresher* was at a depth of more than eighty-four hundred feet. It is believed that her loss was caused by the collapse of a fitting under great force, allowing water to penetrate the hull with unbelievable pressure.

That year, because of the loss of the *Thresher,* attack nuclear submarines were restricted to depths much closer to the surface than originally planned, and the program developed became known as "SubSafe."

Five years went by. The *Thresher* incident began to fade in the minds of those directing the activities of attack nuclear submarines, and all seemed to be going smoothly. Then came the loss of the *Scorpion,* the fifth United States war vessel of that name.

Incidentally, the first two *Scorpions* were sailing craft and became casualties of the War of 1812. On August 21, 1814, the first *Scorpion* was destroyed to prevent her falling into enemy hands. The British on Lake Erie captured the second *Scorpion* later that same year.

The steamer *Aurora* became the third *Scorpion* in 1847, fighting in the Mexican War as a gunboat.

In 1898 the steam yacht *Sovereign,* owned by M. C. D. Borden of Fall River, was purchased for the United States for $300,000 and became the gunboat *Scorpion,* the fourth of her name. She participated in the blockade of Santiago, Cuba. On December 10, 1906, the *Scorpion* collided with both the *Rhode Island* and the *Missouri* while in charge of Lieutenant Commander Frank W. Kellog in attempting to make the dock at the Charlestown Navy Yard. Later, after repairs, she was sent to Constantinople. In World War I she was interned while in Turkey, and in 1927 the fourth *Scorpion* was mustered out of the service.

Launched in 1959, the nuclear-powered 3,075-ton submarine *Scorpion* was a proud vessel carrying out her duties in the service. After a thorough examination in May 1964, she returned to her duties. In the summer of 1967 the 256-foot craft was dry-docked, at the end of which time a few minor faults were corrected. She began new trials the following October with a crew of ninety-nine men. The *Scorpion* was scheduled to arrive from the Mediterranean at the Norfolk Navy Yard by one o'clock in the afternoon of May 27, 1968. Her last signal had been from a location off the Azores on the night of the 21st, and it was understood that all was well.

At the time of the *Scorpion's* message there was no escorting vessel. She had been roughly twenty-three hundred miles from Norfolk when she sent it, and the depth of ocean where the *Scorpion* was heading was from one to four miles!

When she did not appear and no further message came she was declared overdue "since 1 P.M. on May 27." Submarines and destroyers were ordered to search the ocean off Norfolk, and thirty aircraft began to fly systematically over the area.

A few days later a combined search was carried out by all available air and sea craft covering 112,000 square miles of the Atlantic Ocean.

It was then reported that four days before the *Scorpion* was scheduled to land at Norfolk, a surface craft had reported that she had sighted an oil slick about 580 miles east of Norfolk.

Immediately planes were ordered to the location, and four naval vessels were directed to the same spot. One of them, the U.S.S. *Hyades,* was cruising at 6:15 in the morning of the 28th of May. At that moment a crewman noticed an orange-colored cylindrical-shaped object floating on the water.

An aircraft in the vicinity flew down in the area of the *Hyades,* but although a line had been attached to the object, those in the plane could not see it. The line had slipped off the object shortly after being attached. Then came the announcement by naval operations that because of its size and shape the line could be associated "with the submarine."

A further hunt for the oil slick failed to discover anything, and many searchers decided that it was possible there had been no oil slick. Quite often the sun hitting a patch of water under certain conditions may suggest an oil slick, but it is really sunlight and water alone.

Several hours later the weather changed. Rough water and forty-knot winds swept the suspected area. Low clouds developed, making visibility extremely unfavorable.

Nothing was found and the days went by. A submarine was then discovered on the sea bottom off Virginia, but when it was later identified as having gone down at the height of World War II, the entire area was abandoned and search near the Azores was resumed.

Eventually all other craft were taken off the search operation, leaving the *Mizar* and the *Bowditch,* oceanographic survey craft, the only vessels in the suspected area.

A sled of steel-pipe framework was now dragged at a speed of one knot close to the bottom by the *Mizar*. Carried aboard the framework were two strobe units invented by Professor Harold E. Edgerton of the Massachusetts Institute of Technology and another invention of his, a special Edgerton camera. The camera was nicknamed "Fish." It had coverage of 120 degrees, with the light provided by the strobe unit.*

On October 29, 1968, pictures taken by the "Fish" revealed the stricken submarine *Scorpion* lying on the bottom some distance off the Azores, about ten thousand feet below the surface of the Atlantic. Various pictures taken of the craft were clear enough to show the searchers much of identifiable nature. A mooring line could be made out protruding from its stowage locker into the buoy cavity. Also seen were the main tank vents, two hatches into the superstructure, and damaged snorkel exhaust piping. One picture showed in great detail objects on the rocky bottom identified as portions of the *Scorpion*'s hull, photographed some distance away from the sunken craft.

Thus, for all purposes, the most extensive search for a submarine in the history of the United States Navy or any other navy had come to a conclusion.

It is not generally known that on May 10, 1968, eleven days before her final message, the *Scorpion* had encountered a Soviet destroyer in the Mediterranean. All the guns of the Russian craft had been "trained on" the submarine less than one hundred feet away. Of course, there was no conceivable manner in which the Soviet craft could have attached anything to the American submarine which met disaster a relatively short time later, but many have discussed the possibility.

*When I took Dr. Edgerton and his M.I.T. summer-school class around Boston Harbor on the excursion motorvessel *Bay State* a few years ago, he told me that the future possibilities for strobe lights and cameras were fantastic.

Torpedoman Third Class Robert P. Violetti wrote to his mother in Broomall, Pennsylvania, concerning the encounter, and the possibility was later referred to by several retired naval officers as worthy of consideration.

Not only was the destroyer on a secret mission when the disaster took place, but the Navy probe concerning the mystery of what happened to the submarine itself became a seven-man secret court of inquiry.

Two days after the missing sub was due in port, on Wednesday, May 29, 1968, at 8:28 p.m., a single message, using the code name for the *Scorpion*, was received by several craft. The message stated:

ANY STATION THIS NETWORK. THIS IS [SCORPION].

(Instead of the name *Scorpion*, the code word was given). Declared a hoax later, the message was "dastardly", a naval officer stated, giving false hope to scores of relatives of the ninety-nine men aboard the *Scorpion*.

The official information released to the public on November 10 reported that a search involving almost six thousand men and four hundred ships and planes had successfully come to a conclusion.

On January 3, 1969, three distinct possibilities concerning the cause of the disaster were suggested and publicized. One was that crewmen might have panicked when some minor problem had developed, pushed the wrong button or grasped the wrong fulcrum or hit the wrong lever. Another was that a torpedo might have attached itself to the submarine, improbably at the time of the encounter with the Russian destroyer, while the third involved the failure of a pipe similar to that on the *Thresher*. It is known that after the Navy reported the loss of the *Thresher*, the Portsmouth investigation revealed that fourteen percent of the silver brazed joints had substandard bonds. When the Navy heard this, nothing was done, so the Portsmouth Yard simply stopped checking. The *Scorpion* could have had similar trouble.

Whatever the cause, it is apparent that the service of American youth and men aboard such a weapon of war as a submarine will, because of its very nature, become more and more dangerous and perilous as the years go by. In fact, as Captain W. M. Nicholson, head of the Deep Submergence Systems Project, stated shortly after the *Scorpion* tragedy occurred, "We all recognize that if a submarine is lost in deep water, there is nothing that can be done about it."

A memorial service was held for the men of the *Scorpion* on the steps of the historic Massachusetts State House in Boston on June 18, 1968, with the House and Senate meeting in joint session.

The former commanding officer of the submarine, Captain Norman B. Bessac of Cohasset, spoke of the *Scorpion:* "I like to look back to gayer days when a band played as she was born and joined our fleet."

Governor John A. Volpe of Massachusetts told the assemblage that "Massachusetts joins with the Navy and families with sympathy for the loss of our country's finest men." Senate President Maurice A. Donahue stated that the gathering honored "the bravery of those men who went to the bottom of the seas that offer no protection."

House Speaker Robert H. Quinn, in his eulogy at the memorial for those aboard the *Scorpion,* said that "our minds on this occasion are filled with thoughts of the officers and men in the submarine service. The crew were lost while pursuing new frontiers in science and in defense of our country in a nuclear age. They were warriors in peacetime. The men died mysteriously in the wisdom of God."

4

The Palomares Incident

It all began on Monday, January 17, 1966, when two planes of the United States Air Force were carrying out a refueling operation over the Spanish Mediterranean coast at Palomares, a small Iberian village of about twelve hundred souls.

One plane was a jet tanker, the other a B-52 carrying atomic bombs. The tanker was refueling the B-52, and all was in order. The refueling had begun at eleven minutes past ten that morning.

Suddenly an engine on the B-52 caught fire and exploded. The blaze leaped to the jet tanker, whose crew could do nothing to take action in time. The tanker caught fire and both aircraft went out of control, starting to fall. A short time later they both hit the ground, their wreckage scattering over a large area of land and sea.

Although several of the crew opened their parachutes and saved their lives, seven others met death in the air. All possible armament had been jettisoned.

Five miles out to sea, a fishing craft, the *Manuela Orts Simo,* was cruising, when suddenly Captain Francisco Simo

Orts noticed a parachute carrying a cylinder-shaped object falling toward him from out of the sky. The parachute and the cylinder hit the water a short distance away and immediately sank to the bottom. The captain of the fishing craft took a careful check of his position at the time and then was startled when another parachute, then another, and still another began to descend toward him. Each of the three had a man attached to the chute.

Fluttering toward the sea, all three parachutists landed in the water close to Orts, and he started at once to rescue the men. Soon all were aboard his craft. Again he took careful sights of his position and then sped toward shore with the three rescued airmen.

As the hours and then the days went by, hundreds of officers and enlisted men began to converge on the accident area. Soon many scientists of renown joined them. Nevertheless, at this time the U.S. government gave only the barest minimum of facts connected with the terrifying disaster.

Finally, on Thursday, January 20, three days after the event, the United States issued a cautious statement that "nuclear armaments" had been carried on the B-52.

Officially, the government admitted that one bomb, and only one, had been aboard the B-52, although it was later stated that within eighteen hours of the crash three atomic bombs had been recovered from the disaster.

Each bomb was capable, if detonated, of going off with a force 1,250 times more powerful than the bomb which had desolated Hiroshima. If even one of them had exploded upon contact with the earth, everything within an eight-mile flash-point would have been wiped out!

Gradually the news became known to the general public all around the world that a nuclear bomb was probably in the waters of the Mediterranean Sea off the coast of Spain.

Officially, an Air Force statement explained that there was

no danger to "public health or safety." Nevertheless, the statement did nothing to allay the fears of countless millions all over the world. In spite of terrific agitation, the United States did not relieve those fears, and so pressure naturally continued from nations everywhere. A statement of truth regarding the disaster was requested.

Possibly the most definite comment made during this period was by the official information officer connected with the incident whose duty it was to be the liaison between the Navy and the press of the world.

"I have no comment to make about anything, and I cannot comment on why I have to say 'no comment.' "

Incidentally, whenever any ordnance or possession of the United States Air Force is lost in the sea it becomes the task of the United States Navy, if possible, to recover it. The Navy was immediately assigned to locate the missing atomic bomb, but all costs connected with finding it were charged to the Air Force. When it is considered that the total expenditure of funds connected with finding the missing bomb eventually totaled more than any other effort of its type anywhere, $84,500,000, the operation should make every one of us thoughtful.

Given the enormity of the problem ahead, those responsible for finding the bomb realized that they would have to use all possible help in any field at all.

Rear Admiral Roy Swanson, in charge of the entire project, started intensive action in recruiting the vitally needed aid. Announcing that the salvage operations in the Mediterranean Sea would henceforth be known as the SALOPS MED, the admiral put the project into the highest gear possible.

Navy salvage superintendent Commander William Searle now aimed all his efforts toward this objective. The first craft to arrive on the scene was the tug *Kiowa*, which reached the area on January 18, 1966. Three days later the tug was followed by the mine sweepers *Sagacity* and *Pinnacle,* and the greatest hunt in the history of the marine world began.

Other craft arrived almost at once. They were the landing ship *Fort Snelling,* the destroyer *MacDonough,* the rescue craft *Petrel,* the mine sweepers *Skill* and *Nimble,* and the oiler *Nespelen.*

Rear Admiral William S. Guest was put in charge of the salvage operation on January 23, and the government gave him the authority to do anything possible which would result in bringing up the missing bomb.

He sent for the new Westinghouse ocean-bottom scanning sonar, with a shape similar to the conventional torpedo and designed to be towed roughly thirty feet above the sea bottom. This sonar scanning device had the ability to proceed thousands of feet below the surface at a speed of one knot and was built to scan a path 520 feet wide on the bottom.

Admiral Guest knew that there was another device or machine at the Naval Ordnance testing station in Pasadena, California, consisting of three combined telescope cameras which had already been tested to resist pressures as far down as two thousand feet. He ordered the device sent by the fastest means possible.

There was also a sea scanner developed by Honeywell Corporation which automatically indicated depth, direction, and the distance of objects spotted. Admiral Guest also ordered the scanner to arrive by the quickest available means.

Even now civilian observers were given no hint as to what Guest was looking for, but most of them had a strong suspicion. In the United States the awesome news of the missing atomic bomb became known unofficially within a relatively short time.

Of course, nothing official was even hinted. Day after day went by on the scene, and although scores of possible locations were thoroughly searched, there were no favorable results.

Admiral Guest learned about the fishing craft at the scene of the incident and planned to check Captain Orts' assertion that he could place a fix on where the bomb entered the water. However, there were scores upon scores of testimonials in other areas, and Guest decided that the evidence should be approached in systematic fashion, with the Orts investigation taking a logical place in the order of activity.

On January 26, he ordered the survey craft *Dutton* to chart the bottom wherever Captain Orts directed. That same day Admiral Guest carefully studied the entire report of the fisherman.

Admiral Guest realized that the bottom ground where Orts indicated the bomb sank was woefully broken up. Gigantic underwater canyons cut through massive areas of rockbed which reached down thousands of feet. In many cases mud and silt piled up on the rocks to add to the search problem.

However, results were beginning to show. Many hopeful contacts had been made by the *Dutton,* and it was imperative that other craft be brought in to examine the evidence. The bathyscaphe *Trieste II,* a small, cigar-shaped submersible called *Deep-Jeep,* the *Alvin,* and the *Aluminaut* were all considered.

The *Alvin,* twenty-two feet long, displaced about thirteen tons and could go down to six thousand feet and stay a full twenty-four hours. It had a fifteen-mile range at four knots, carried a crew of two men, was equipped with sonar telephone, magnetic compass, scanning sonar, and closed-circuit television. Usually attached was a grappling claw, which was not aboard at the time. The *Alvin* was sent to the scene immediately, with the grappling claw to follow.

The *Aluminaut,* constructed by the Reynolds Aluminum

Corporation, was fifty-one feet long and displaced eighty-one tons. It had been built to go down fifteen thousand feet and had been tested satisfactorily for sixty-five hundred feet. It cruised at almost four knots and had underwater phones, lighting equipment, continuous transmission, frequency modulated scanning sonar, TV camera, gyro compass, and a pair of nine-foot mechanical arms, which were not on board at the time.

Ocean Systems, Inc., had built a submersible capable of going down six hundred feet. Her name was the *Cubmarine.* She could stay at the bottom for six hours and was about to enter the picture.

When the *Aluminaut* arrived on February 9, Admiral Guest was aboard his flagship, the *Boston,* where he received the officers of the *Aluminaut.* By this time scores of contacts on the bottom had been made in the area, and every single possibility had to be examined.

By February 15, after weather delays, both the *Aluminaut* and the *Alvin* were ready for testing, but two important contact discoveries had to be examined first. Meanwhile, another B-52 dropped a dummy bomb in the area to find out what might have happened to the other, but the second bomb also vanished.

Another arrival at this time was the underwater tracking research craft *Mizar,* carrying valuable tracking equipment.

The two contact discoveries were now examined at the bottom and found to be wing fragments from the B-52. Meanwhile, two other craft arrived, the tug *Luiseno,* and a nineteen-hundred-ton salvage craft named *Hoist,* also part of the Navy. They were ideally built for heavy salvage work. At this time the Reynolds Aluminum group sent the *Privateer* to participate. Perfectly equipped to work along with other craft, her sonar system could communicate underwater with the *Aluminaut* at a distance up to seven and a half miles.

On March 1 the government finally announced that there actually was one atomic bomb still lost. Also, the government stated that two of the three bombs recovered on land had split their casings and exploded their TNT loads! Vital components of the bomb, the Plutonium 239 and U-235, had impregnated a large amount of farmland in the area, necessitating topsoil stripping and the packing of that topsoil into about five thousand fifty-five-gallon oil drums and then shipping it away.

Incredibly, the radioactive life of the material spilled onto the Palomares farmland area was more than twenty-four milleniums, or 24,400 years in time!

Days upon days now elapsed with all the ships and underwater craft testing contact after contact at the sea bottom, but the atomic bomb was not found. The report of Francisco Simo Orts had been studied extensively, but still awaited actual on-the-bottom activity. Orts still was sure where the bomb had gone down, and he knew the searching craft would never find it where it had not gone down.

Then came the moment when the searchers turned to Orts. The Spanish fisherman and his ability could be compared to the lobster fishermen of Maine and Massachusetts, who are able to take a bearing on land in a few different directions and drop their traps with unerring accuracy. Orts knew he was right as to his location fix on the bomb parachute and the bomb itself. The Simo area would soon pay off. The scientists went aboard the *Manuela Simo,* with the *Alvin* standing by. One day the officials waited until Orts went below, then they moved the *Simo.* They hadn't fooled Orts, however, for when he came up on deck again he took a sighting of the surroundings and accused the investigators of moving the craft, and they confessed.

Orts now announced he was over the parachute and bomb site. The *Alvin* began a careful search of the Orts area, starting at about 10:30 on the morning of March 15. The great moment was not long in arriving. At about 11:50 that morning, when at 2,550 feet down, those on the *Alvin* sighted a section of the colored silk cloth parachute which had floated the atom bomb down into the sea near Orts' craft.

Unfortunately, the bomb and the parachute were in a terribly dangerous underwater location, in the midst of rocky cliffs, crevices, and abysses which formed the sea bottom there. Even a slight jolt might detonate the TNT inside the bomb. The *Alvin* remained for the next four hours taking pictures of the parachute and the bomb, and then came up to the surface, her work well done.

Admiral Guest now decided that he would add a touch of humor to the serious situation, and so he named the parachute for his son Douglas and the bomb itself Robert, for his other son.

As the *Alvin* rose to the surface, the *Aluminaut* went down to the scene at once. She carried with her a sonar transponder to be attached to the parachute or bomb, and it would act as a homing device. The transponder took three hours to attach, but even then efforts to lift Robert failed, and the bomb buried itself deeper and deeper into the mud and silt of the area.

On March 19 Admiral Guest ordered a securing anchor hooked into the parachute, but a gale with thirty-five-knot winds arrived and stopped the action for several days. On March 23 the *Alvin* went down again to attempt another hooking of the anchor.

The work began, but suddenly the bomb started to move, sliding three feet closer to the crevice. The *Alvin* was then replaced by the *Aluminaut,* and the salvage efforts continued.*

Guest decided that *CURV,* an invention of Howard Talkington, should now be sent for. The initials for the invention stood for Cable-controlled Underwater Research Vessel. The invention possessed a claw, it could go down 2,000 feet, and it had almost every new idea so vital to an operation of this type.

Arriving on March 25, those on the *CURV* were just in time to learn that the *Alvin* had slid down on the bomb itself and was then engulfed by the parachute. Successfully backing off, the *Alvin* pushed the anchor into the parachute folds and then hooked the folds.

The *Hoist,* which I mentioned earlier, was then sent down to pull the atomic bomb up the side of the steep underwater slope to a safer location. All seemed to be going well, but suddenly the strong nylon line broke in two. It had been sawed apart by a roughness in the anchor flukes.

The bomb plunged down the seventy-degree slope, then luckily bounced over the crevice to vanish into a muddy area on the other side of the gully. This was all watched by the men on the *Alvin,* who became utterly discouraged.

Now on a shelving area about 2,850 feet down, as indicated by the transponder, the bomb was still attached to the parachute. Actually it was in a precarious perch on a thirty-five-degree slope just above a rocky crevice forty-two hundred feet in depth.

To make matters worse, stormy weather now prevailed,

---

*If any of my readers has ever attempted to dig clams or quahogs in knee-deep water, he probably remembers the roiled water once he has dug his clam fork into the sand or mud, necessitating a wait until the water clears. On a gigantically larger scale, it was the same problem. Each attempt to hook the parachute brought enough silt to shroud the scene for at least half an hour.

and all efforts were abandoned. It wasn't until April 1 that the *Alvin* dared to go down again. The crew discovered that the bomb had vanished into sliding mud. By April 5, however, the cameras aboard *CURV* revealed that Douglas, the parachute named by Admiral Guest, had been uncovered and was then in plain sight.

CURV now dropped cautiously down until it was less than three feet away from the parachute. It then squeezed its claw into the silk of the parachute. The parachute recovery line now started for the surface.

It was the *Alvin*'s turn to take over. Unfortunately, the bomb started to slide lower and the *Alvin* dropped down into the parachute, whose folds soon enveloped it. Now there were only four hours left in the *Alvin*'s batteries, and the craft would have to free itself. The *Alvin* began maneuvering back and forth. Suddenly came a moment of liberation and the *Alvin* was able to pull away from the chute.

Getting back to the surface, those aboard the *Alvin* were ready for another try by ten o'clock the next morning. The *Alvin* went down again. The crew of the *Alvin* succeeded in attaching their line to the top of the parachute. Then foul weather arrived, and all efforts stopped again.

Finally, at an hour after midnight on April 7, *CURV* descended on its cable control and quickly caught itself in the parachute. The crisis was at hand. With the bomb still acting fitfully on the sea bottom, Admiral Guest made his decision. He notified all listeners that he would attempt to bring up everything—*CURV,* the parachute, and, hopefully, the bomb—all on the cable.

Underwater submersible *CURV* now started rising, connected with the parachute and bomb. Both followed, moving at a modest speed of twenty-seven feet every minute. At 8:19 *CURV* swung free, and finally Robert, the atom bomb, was only one hundred feet down.

Scuba divers now descended to the suspended bomb and secured it around the middle. Soon all was ready. Slowly but surely the atomic bomb was lifted toward the surface of the Mediterranean Sea.

At exactly fifteen minutes before nine o'clock that April 7th morning, the ten-foot bomb broke the water's surface. It had been on the bottom not quite eighty days. The scuba divers now disconnected the electric plugs from the silvery monster, thus defusing the detonating charge of TNT inside.

The bomb was slowly raised into the air and placed aboard the *Petrel.* Francisco Simo Orts rightly became the man of the hour.

Paying scant attention to him at first, the Navy had searched for the bomb for fifty-eight days at a cost of well over a million dollars a day. Then, moving to the location the fisherman already knew about, where Orts had watched the bomb parachute hit the water, the *Alvin* had gone down and located the bomb in less than an hour and twenty minutes! Never before in history had so much money been spent for a salvage operation.

PART 5

Pirates, Patriots,
and Privateers

1

Ocean Born Mary

Henniker, New Hampshire, called by many a little "cross-roads village," prides itself on being the "only Henniker on earth." In 1768 Governor Benning Wentworth* granted the town a charter. Because of his old friend John Henniker, whom he had met in England, he named the village Henniker.

In Henniker, near a junction between State Road 114 and the Gulf Road, stands the Ocean Born Mary house. About three miles from the intersection, the ancient dwelling actually is the center of a world of its own. Well I remember my talks with Mr. Roy, the occupant of the residence more than a quarter century ago, and the tiny photographs he made and sold. According to the Reverend Robert Hallam Lewis, both Mr. Roy and his mother are buried in the Roy private cemetery across the street from the Ocean Born Mary house.

I also recall the discussions I had in Boston with George

*In my book *True Tales and Curious Legends* I tell the story of Governor Wentworth who at the age of sixty-three married a young girl of twenty.

Allan England, who believed that if he removed the giant hearthstone in the Ocean Born Mary house, he would find a substantial pirate treasure. He did lift the giant stone, but absolutely nothing was underneath. Later others claimed that a skeleton had been under the stone, but Mr. England did not see it.

It is only fair to state that there are many versions of the Ocean Born Mary story, but I now record the original story, unembellished by the passing of time.

Around the year 1718 James Wilson and Elizabeth Fulton were married in Ireland and decided to go to America where they planned to settle. In June 1720 they sailed away from Londonderry, Ireland, hoping that eventually they would reach Londonderry, New Hampshire.

From the very beginning the voyage was fraught with unexpected events. First the vessel sailed into stormy weather. Then, Elizabeth's baby was born prematurely. Finally, on July 28, when the weather moderated, a ship appeared on the horizon and began to chase the America-bound passenger craft. Soon there was no doubt that the pursuers were pirates.

The captain of the emigrant craft hastily called the crew and the leading members of the ship's company to a conference during which it was decided that resistance was useless, for there were not enough able-bodied men aboard to fight the pirates.

A few hours later, as the oncoming vessel fluttered her skull and crossbones from the mainmast, her crew fired a cannon across the bow of their victim, which immediately hove to, while the pirates put over several small boats.

In a short time the attackers were swarming aboard the passenger ship, shouting coarse piratical oaths as they scrambled over the rail. Then the men, trained to kill and plunder, fell upon the awe-stricken crew and passengers, not one of whom offered any resistance. Soon every man was bound hand and foot, but so far no one had been killed. In a wild scramble for plunder, such articles as could be transferred to the pirate vessel were piled together. Yelling and screaming, the marauders rushed back and forth, unmindful of the entreaties of their victims.

While his followers were carrying on this lawless work, the captain of the buccaneers, whose hardened face revealed not the slightest sign of mercy, went below to search the officers' quarters, expecting to find some of his richest booty there. Bursting in the door, he discovered Elizabeth Wilson lying in the berth. The surprise of this piratical commander was evidenced by his long stare at the woman in the cabin bunk and the bundle at her side.

"Who are you, and why are you here?" he demanded.

The terrified mother uncovered the newly born infant and held the baby girl up for the intruder's inspection.

All appearance of his piratical character swiftly left him and a kindly look swept over his countenance. The pirate advanced carefully to the mother's side.

"A girl?" he questioned.

"Yes," she answered timidly.

"Has she been named?"

"Not yet."

"Good."

Thereupon the pirate went back to the cabin door and ordered his men to stop all further action until he should return to the deck. Then, he again approached the side of the berth where the mother and her baby lay. All of his original thoughts of plunder and murder were forgotten. Almost reverently he took the tiny, unresisting hand of the baby in his own.

"If I may name this little girl for another I once knew, I promise life and safety to every passenger on this ship. On that condition, may I name the girl?"

"Yes."

The dark-browed outlaw of the sea bowed his head low over the mother and child while he whispered softly the name that seemed sacred to him: "Mary."

When he released the little hand, his tears were on it, while a strange light glowed from his countenance. A moment later he was gone, leaving the mother overwhelmed by the emotion he had shown.

Upon reaching the deck, the outlaw ordered his men to unbind all the captives and restore the valuables to the places from which they had been taken.

Surprised, disappointed, and grumbling, the pirates nevertheless obeyed their leader, and a short time later the vessel was free of her unwelcome visitors. While unable to comprehend what had happened to make the attackers leave, the captain of the passenger craft gave orders to get underway.

The respite, however, was of short duration, for it was suddenly noticed that the pirate commander was coming back in one of the small boats! This time, however, he was alone with two oarsmen, so the fears of the passengers were somewhat mitigated. As soon as he came on board, alone now, the pirate went directly below to the captain's cabin. Under his arm he carried a package of considerable size.

With mingled emotions Elizabeth Wilson watched him enter. To her surprise the visitor then unfolded before her startled gaze the most beautiful parcel of brocaded silk she had ever seen.

"Let Mary make her wedding gown from this," he said simply.

Then, kissing the tiny hand of the now sleeping baby, he stole silently out of the cabin.

The vessel continued on her voyage, eventually arriving in Boston where the passengers left the ship. The Wilsons carried out their plans and settled in the Londonderry, New Hampshire, area. For many years July 28 was religiously observed in the Wilson family out of remembrance to the christening of Ocean Born Mary, as she became known, a day of deliverance for herself and her friends from the pirates.

Left a widow in the course of time, Elizabeth Wilson married again. This time her husband was James Clark, a great-great-grandparent of Horace Greeley. As Mrs. Clark, she spent the remainder of her life in Londonderry.

Ocean Born Mary became a bride on her eighteenth birthday. She married Thomas Wallace and her wedding gown was made from the pirate's silk. Nor was she the only one to wear this wonderful dress, for, although she had no daughter of her own, it was handed down to granddaughter and great-granddaughter to be worn on similar occasions. Ocean Born Mary lived the last years of her long and happy life in Henniker and her grave is in the cemetery there located close to the railroad station.

In the year 1946, L. M. A. Roy was living in the Ocean Born Mary House. When I visited him that summer he told me that Captain Kidd was the pirate who boarded the Irish immigrant craft and gave Mary the bolt of silken cloth. I explained that there were only two things wrong with this story. Kidd, of course, never was a pirate, but a privateer. Furthermore, he was hanged in 1701, nineteen years before the encounter of the mysterious marauder with Ocean Born Mary.

Mr. Roy informed me that the same pirate who named the Wilson girl Mary sailed up the Merrimac River and the Contoocook until he reached Henniker. The buccaneer had brought along his followers, slaves, and carpenters, and there he built the Ocean Born Mary house. At the same time, according to Mr. Roy, he brought a large treasure along with him which he buried in the vicinity.

A short time later the pirate was found, with a cutlass run

through his body, in the grove behind the mansion, and he was buried nearby. Many say that the large hearthstone in the kitchen of the house marked his tomb but, as I indicated, it is empty at the present time.

When Ocean Born Mary died in the Eagle Room of the Henniker mansion in 1814, she was ninety-four years of age. A visit to her house is a never-to-be-forgotten treat. Built after 1760, it is a typical sea captain's residence. A fragment of the original silk given to Ocean Born Mary by the pirate is reputedly still on exhibition.

2

Newport Pirate Tom Tew

On August 22, 1944, a lady passenger aboard the boat which ran from Boston to Provincetown, Mrs. Pauline Johnson Sims, was reading my book *Storms and Shipwrecks* and came across on the jacket that I was interested in pirates.

She wrote to me that afternoon to explain that she was descended from a New England pirate named Thomas Tew. I answered her letter, and a lively correspondence began. This eventually led to her appearance on my Six Bells Show over WNAC, a Boston radio station, and a later attempt on her part to purchase a treasure chest from a Cape Codder who traced the chest from pirate Tew himself.

Trouble developed with the details of purchasing the treasure chest, and Mrs. Sims asked me to journey to Cape Cod, get the chest, and pay the balance which Mrs. Sims was said to owe. After several trips, I completed the transaction, wrote to Mrs. Sims, and discovered that in the interim she had died. No one else in the Sims family had the slightest interest in the chest, so I brought the Thomas Tew treasure chest back to Marshfield with me, and it is still in Marshfield.

One of Mrs. Sim's ancestors, Richard Tew, hailing from Mardford, England, settled at Newport, Rhode Island, in 1640. Elected a deputy there, he soon became well known and highly respected. Fifty-one years later his adventuresome young grandson, Thomas, sailed into Bermuda eager to acquire a share in the sloop *Amity,* a vessel owned by prominent residents there.

Thomas Tew succeeded in getting himself appointed captain of the craft and obtained a privateering commission, after which he enlisted a crew and departed from Bermuda. Once out on the high seas, Tew suggested to his men that they turn pirates. They agreed, shouting, "A gold chain or a wooden leg—we'll stand by you."

Tew soon captured a rich prize with fabulous treasures aboard. It was an Arabian vessel, and when the booty had been divided each member of the crew received three thousand pounds as his share.

After a visit to Madagascar, the *Amity* sailed toward America, by chance meeting another pirate vessel under the command of the infamous Captain Mission. Mission, who had established a pirate Utopia at Madagascar called Libertalia, invited Tew for a visit there. The Rhode Islander enjoyed what he discovered at Libertalia and lived for some time at the pirate kingdom. Finally he sailed out on a mission to capture slaving vessels. Freeing the slaves, he brought them back to Libertalia where they were given equal privileges with the pirates. Tew and Mission claimed that they wished to build up a strong, faithful island empire free from class distinctions.

The Newport pirate's next venture was to chart and survey the treacherous Madagascar coast, a task which took four months. Although he did an excellent job, not a single copy of his chart exists today.

Tew then decided to establish a trade route between Newport, Rhode Island, and the pirate kingdom. He was already a very prosperous man when he sailed away from Libertalia. He set his course first for the island of Bermuda, but a bad gale which sprung his mast forced him off the course. After beating about for two weeks he decided to head directly for his Newport home, which he reached a week later. Despite his lawless occupation he was received with much respect on arriving ashore, especially when the townsfolk learned how wealthy he had become.

Waiting to hear from him in Bermuda, however, were the five co-owners of the *Amity*. Included in their membership was one of the governor's council! Tew at once sent a dispatch to them, asking for an agent to come to Newport to receive their shares of the vessel's trip. When Captain Starrs, the representative appointed by the Bermuda partners, sailed into Newport Harbor, he discovered that some of the money had been buried by Tew, while the rest was deposited in Boston. The total amount constituted substantial profits for all concerned. Governor's Councilman William Outerbridge became richer by over three thousand pounds, receiving his share in "Lyon dollars and Arabian gold." Tew himself was able to bank around eight thousand pounds for his efforts on the high seas. He brought so many Arabian gold pieces into Newport that for a time these sizable coins, worth twice the value of Spanish dollars, were common not only there but in New York as well!

The captain journeyed to Boston to apply for a new privateering commission, but the cautious commissioners refused his request. Undaunted, Tew easily persuaded them to change their minds with a bribe of five hundred pounds. Armed now with this authority to capture French ships, Tew went to New York where he located one Frederick Phillips, of whom he had heard. Phillips, known as one of the "brethren," at once declared himself interested in Tew's contem-

plated voyage to Madagascar. The ship *Frederick* was outfit-
ted and made ready for sea, and a few weeks later Tew sailed
with a full cargo for the port of Libertalia. After a relatively
uneventful journey he reached the Madagascar coast.

Pleased with Tew's success, Captain Mission welcomed
him heartily, and the rich cargo of New England merchan-
dise was brought ashore and distributed. After a few weeks
had gone by, Mission suggested to Tew that a cruise to the
Red Sea might prove lucrative to both of them. For this
purpose Mission furnished two large ships, each manned by
two hundred and fifty men, and the voyage began.

Off the Arabian coast the two captains fell in with a ship
of the Great Mogul, packed with sixteen hundred pilgrims
on the way to Mecca. Although the Great Mogul's vessel
carried more than one hundred guns, there was no real force
to man them, and when the pirates sailed into battle against
them the pilgrims offered little effective resistance. Boarding
the ship, the pirates cut their way through the passengers,
and the encounter was soon over.

Not one of the buccaneers was killed, and they promptly
started a systematic examination of their prize. After stripping the vessel of all treasure, they decided to consider taking
some of the females on board back to their island stronghold.
It seems that the lack of suitable women at the pirate Shan-
gri-La was one of the few things which caused discontent
among the men. After declaring their marital status, the
unmarried girls were placed in one part of the ship while the
wives were congregated elsewhere. About one hundred single girls between twelve and eighteen years of age could be
accommodated without trouble back in Libertalia, and despite the entreaties of the Mecca-bound Muhammadans, the
captive maidens were removed to the pirate vessels.

The return journey to Libertalia began with the pilgrim
ship in company. In port, as the Great Mogul's craft was a

poor sailor, she was taken apart. She had yielded countless treasures in diamonds, silks, and gold, and her hundred guns were mounted in two batteries near the harbor's mouth. Except for the hapless unmarried girls, the survivors of the capture were allowed to return home as best they could.

Affairs were now progressing in such a favorable manner that certain features of the pirate colony resembled a glorified Brook Farm project. The prosperous settlement was by this time strongly fortified, and a farming community was being developed in the rear of the village where several scores of acres of land were being cultivated. Three hundred head of sturdy black cattle grazed on the rolling fields nearby, and a great commercial pier was completed. Each pirate had chosen his own location for a home, which accommodated not one but two, three, or four of the wives of his particular choice.

One beautiful morning some months after Thomas Tew had returned from America, one of the pirate sloops came sailing into the harbor chased by no less than five great ships of the Portuguese navy. It was a dangerous moment, but the pirates were equal to the occasion. Every cannon around the entire harbor system of fortifications was manned within a few minutes, and when the pursuers drew abeam of the fort, Tew was in command of all the English-speaking pirates on the island while Mission had charge of the other nationalities.

All but one of the five Portuguese warships successfully ran past the outer system of fortifications, but when they reached the inner harbor they received such a merciless pounding that two of the attackers were immediately sunk. Devastating fire was poured into the remaining vessels by the combined efforts of the shore batteries and the pirate ships in the harbor. A third vessel was boarded and taken, while the captains of the two Portuguese men-of-war still afloat, realizing that the battle was lost, ran for the harbor's entrance to escape. They made it successfully, although they were badly damaged, and sailed away. It is said that this engagement became the subject of pirate conversation all over the world for years to come. A pirate stronghold on the Madagascar coast had defeated a fleet of the best ships of the Portuguese navy!

The Newport pirate had acquitted himself well in the fight. As a reward, Tew was now made admiral of the fleet. With this new honor he began to have great dreams of a powerful piratical empire. He suggested a voyage to the Indian Sea to gather new recruits. The colony, he thought, was rich enough, but needed fresh blood.

Leaving Libertalia on board the flagship *Victorie,* with three hundred of the most hardened pirates manning his guns and yards, Tew decided to call on his old quartermaster who had left the *Amity* to settle ashore on another part of the island of Madagascar. The quartermaster, now governor of the area, was pleased to see his former captain again, but declined, as did the others in his colony, to leave their idyllic settlement. They were living in comfort and security with plenty of their treasure still intact, and the governor had no wish to go to sea again. But he asked the Rhode Islander to stay for the afternoon and had a feast prepared for the occasion.

Suddenly, at the height of the banquet, a storm arose to churn the waters into a frightful gale, throwing the *Victorie* ashore on a rugged promontory near the settlement. All of the pirates aboard were drowned in full sight of their captain, who could give them no assistance.

This sudden change in the fortunes of the Newport pirate came as a great shock to Tew, who not only was left without a ship but had no means of communicating with the home port.

Two sloops sailed into the quartermaster's harbor some weeks later, and gave the Rhode Islander great happiness. His joy was short-lived, however, for Captain Mission had tragic news of his own. After Tew's departure, another pirate vessel, the *Bijoux,* had also left the settlement with a large force of buccaneers aboard. Probably through the offices of a spy, it became known to the natives that the pirate stronghold had been seriously weakened by the absence of the two ships. Seizing the opportunity, they secretly prepared to attack Libertalia.

Tew was told that the invasion of the colony had started in the dead of the night. As the natives stormed the settlement, men, women, and children were slaughtered without mercy. The weakened garrison proved no match for the determined Madagascars, who had old scores to settle. Captain Mission, seeing the way the battle was going, fled to the waterfront, where he boarded a sloop. Hoisting sail, he and a small group hastily left the harbor. Another sloop later got away, but only forty-five pirates survived the onslaught. In spite of his hasty exit, Mission departed with a substantial amount of diamonds and gold.

After the pirate captains had commiserated with each other, the Newport pirate proposed a new journey to America where they could settle unmolested in either Newport or New York. But Mission claimed that he was homesick for his family in France and would have to return to the continent before deciding. He gave Tew one of the sloops, and divided his diamonds and gold. The two parted company, Mission sailing away with a crew of fifteen, while Tew set out from Madagascar with thirty-four Englishmen.

More trouble lay ahead. Running into a violent storm on the way to the Cape of Good Hope, Captain Mission's sloop went down within a short distance of Tew's vessel, and the Newport pirate was unable to save his friend. It was such a terrific storm that not a single pirate could be saved from the raging seas.

The rest of the journey around the Cape of Good Hope and across the Atlantic to America was more or less uneventful, with the sloop arriving safely in Newport Harbor a few weeks later. Here Tew divided his treasure with the members of his crew who, it has been said, hied off to Boston, where they "shewed themselves publicly" on the streets of that sedate city.

The captain, however, settled down quietly at Newport, where he lived in peace. Gradually others of his crew returned to Newport. One of them, Thomas Jones, married Penelope Goulden and remained in Rhode Island.

Benjamin Fletcher, the governor of New York, was a good friend of Thomas Tew, and could often be seen with the notorious pirate on the streets of New York, nor did he mind dining with him at his palatial home. Of course, Tew had many dealings in New York, where he disposed of a large share of his uncut diamonds. Governor Fletcher, like some other colonial governors, was always ready to turn "an honest penny." And so it was that when Tew presented himself at the governor's mansion on November 4, 1694, to apply for a privateering commission to go on a voyage which his crew had urged, Fletcher readily consented—for the payment of three hundred pounds.

A few days later the Rhode Island captain sailed from Newport Harbor aboard the *Amity*. He was joined shortly by two other vessels, one a sloop commanded by Captain Wake, an old pirate pardoned by King James, and the other a brigantine captained by Master Want, Tew's mate on his first trip. Others who made the voyage included Thomas Jones of Newport, who left his wife Penelope at the pier. Tew's fleet was further augmented by the appearance of Captain Glover in a ship from New York. By June 1695 the fleet had reached Liparau Island at the mouth of the Red Sea, where Tew joined the pirate armada of the great and equally famous "Long Ben" Avery.*

A week later twenty-five Arab ships passed their fleet in the dead of night. When Avery heard the news, he started in quick pursuit. Tew's *Amity*, unfortunately, could not match the fast pace which its companion set and fell behind. Meanwhile, Avery came up with a Moorish ship, from which he took sixty thousand pounds in gold and silver. Then another craft was sighted, overhauled, and captured, this time yielding one hundred and eighty thousand pounds to be divided.

It is not known whether or not Captain Tew ever heard of the rich treasure taken from these Moorish ships, but he fell in with another one of the fleet some days later and attacked it. Perhaps his luck had turned or the easygoing life had softened both him and the crew. In any case, when the Moors offered unexpected resistance to the Yankee pirate, Tew realized that he was face to face with defeat that afternoon. Suddenly a shot carried away a portion of his stomach, and, in the words of Daniel Defoe, Tew "held his Bowels with his Hands some small Space; when he dropp'd, it struck such a Terror in his men, that they suffered themselves to be taken, without making Resistance."

And so pirate Thomas Tew died, far from his native Newport, where he had planned to live in peace and comfort during his declining years. I often wonder what happened to the contents of another chest that he left behind, mentioned in the *Calendar of State Papers* for 1696 and 1697. It was so heavy "that six men at the tackles" could hardly hoist it.

More than a dozen descendants of Tom Tew live today in the general vicinity of Newport, Rhode Island, whence their ancestor sailed to plunder the seas more than 280 years ago.

*See my *True Tales of Pirates and Their Gold,* pages 56–67.

3

The Boston Tea Party

The Massachusetts Marine Historical League began celebrating the anniversaries of the Boston Tea Party in 1944. One of the most impressive anniversary parties after the first meeting in 1944 came on the afternoon of December 16, 1972, 199 years after the original affair. On that day a goodly number of the Massachusetts Marine Historical League met with a group of distinguished guests at Kevin's Wharf Restaurant across Fort Point Channel from the actual scene of the 1773 party.

Among those at the head table were Massachusetts Attorney General Robert H. Quinn, City Councilor Gabriele Piemonte, naval historian Asa E. Philips, Jr., and James Turbayne of the Needham Historical Society. It was my pleasure to act as master of ceremonies, and we drank tea from the original Boston Tea Party as we ate a fine meal.

A year later the Marine Historical League members were again present when the 200th Anniversary Commemoration service began on the afternoon of December 16, 1973. During the final hours of daylight they watched patiently as many events of completely extraneous nature occurred near the site of the famed Tea Party. Several acts which had nothing to do with the original Tea Party took place, including a rather degrading demonstration by those of riotous nature during which one performance ridiculed the President of the United States.

As winter darkness fell over the scene, the hour of 6:00 P.M. arrived, the time when the first chest of tea was dropped into Boston Harbor in 1773. Rioters and others who had participated in the afternoon activities of the 200th Anniversary left the area, and the Tea Party plaque became the goal of all who remained. Gathered by the memorial tablet on the Sheraton Building at 470 Atlantic Avenue, twenty-six persons listened as President William Smits spoke briefly of the Marine Historical League's December activities.

The League had visited the little-known Tea Party tablet at Marshfield where some tea had been burned and later had gone to Peak's Island, Maine, where the last survivor of the Tea Party was honored.* Then the League had sponsored a trip to Provincetown, where the location of the fourth Tea Party craft, the shipwrecked brigantine *William,* was reached on schedule.

Now, again, we were about to drink some of the original tea from the Boston Tea Party.

Rain, sleet, and hail had begun to fall, and members of the group shivered and shook as the storm battered those gathered in front of the tablet. Standing on the freezing sidewalk, each of us received a cup containing relatively small portions of the original tea.

Especially uncomfortable were those who earlier had attended a cocktail party indoors which did not call for foul

*David Kennison of Lebanon, Maine, who died in 1852, lived to be 115 and had twenty-two children.

weather gear, and they suffered far more than those who were more or less suitably clad. One young woman was not only shivering and shaking standing there in her dainty costume, but actually was on the verge of collapse.

Finally, with all cups filled, I gave the signal and we drank the hot liquid. As we quaffed it we received some temporary relief from the icy weather, but all agreed on one thing. The taste of the tea was "terrible."

Three months later we really rang the curtain down on the Tea Party anniversary on March 7, 1974, by drinking the tea again at Hubbard's Wharf where in 1774 tea had also been thrown into the harbor, this time from the brig *Fortune*. The unlucky craft lost all her twenty-eight and one-half chests of tea which were dumped into Boston Harbor by sixty men disguised as Indians. On that occasion the time was 8:30 at night.

Contrary to popular belief, tea has not always been a favorite drink for either Europeans or Americans. Actually, the first mention of the delightful liquid was on June 27, 1615, when East India Officer Wickham wrote to another officer of the same company, named Eaton, asking for a pot of the best sort of "chaw."

Even then tea-drinking progress was slow, for it was not until forty-five years later, on September 25, 1660, that diarist Samuel Pepys sent for "a cup of tee," which Pepys records was a "China drink I have never drunk before." This statement indicates that tea was a novelty as late as 1660.

To have a proper perspective concerning the Boston Tea Party, one must go back to the year 1765, when England adopted a strong imperial policy with her colonies and imposed the Stamp Act which placed a tax on newspapers, pamphlets, and legal papers. The colonies objected strenuously, and the Stamp Act was repealed the next year.

In 1767 an aggressive, brilliant politician, Charles Townshend, then heading the British cabinet, proposed and had passed new taxes on paper, glass, lead, painters' colors, and tea. To insure the collection of the taxes, writs of assistance were instituted.

On August 1, 1768, an agreement was made by 211 Boston merchants that for the entire year of 1769 they would refuse to import anything from Great Britain except a few necessities. The agreement emphasized that they would not bring into the country tea, glass, paper, or painters' colors unless the acts were repealed.

The women of New England, possibly forerunners of the Women's Liberation Movement, expressed very strong feelings on the subject. Three hundred of them residing in the North End of Boston agreed not to drink British tea until the revenue acts were repealed. Not wishing to be outdone, on February 12, 1770, 126 other women signed a statement promising not to drink British tea.

The young men of Boston showed their patriotism, in a manner that led to fatal consequences. Late in February 1770, the boys placed an effigy in front of the home of Theophilus Lille. An informer, Ebenezer Richardson, was pelted with stones by a group of the young men and boys, and he answered by firing his musket into the crowd, killing eleven-year-old Christopher Snider and wounding Christopher Gore.*

On February 26 a great funeral was held for young Snider from his Boylston Street home, with five hundred schoolboys and thirteen hundred other people on foot, and a large number of chariots and other vehicles following the coffin to Liberty Tree where the procession rested briefly. Then it continued to the Granary Burial Ground where Snider's gravestone may be identified today. The excitement caused

*Christopher Gore later became governor of Massachusetts.

by this act eventually led to bitter feeling between the British and Americans in Boston, and the soldiers were the particular butt of the rougher element in town.

On March 5, 1770, the Boston Massacre occurred, with five persons dying as the result of what was no more than a street brawl. The effects, however, were just as important and far-reaching as if the affair had been organized. It was a hinge to the door of the Revolution.

On that same March 5, the British Prime Minister, Lord North, ordered the repeal of all the Townshend acts with one small exception, a three-penny tax on tea. Lord North reasoned that as tea was a luxury anyway, a small trifling duty to please British tea merchants would not matter to the Americans.

On May 20, 1773, the Massachusetts House of Representatives appointed a committee of fifteen members, with Samuel Adams as chairman, to observe the acts and resolutions of the British Parliament. The British government insisted firmly on the duty on tea, and the colonists just as firmly insisted that they would not pay it. Nevertheless, there was considerable tea drinking in America, as it was smuggled in from Holland at a price much less than the Britishers demanded. When the tea arrived in America, there was little trouble getting it ashore illegally.

The East India Company was well aware of the smuggling, and on August 30, 1773, decided to have a "showdown." After obtaining a license to export 600,000 pounds of tea, the company accepted the provision that the duty of only three pennies would be paid at the customhouse in America. The price of the tea was so low that in spite of the tax it would be cheaper than the smuggled Dutch tea.

Early in October it became known that there were plans to send four tea ships to Boston, the *Beaver*, the *Eleanor*, the

Dartmouth, and the *William.** Hearing the news, the patriots determined to ask the consignees that they resign their commissions.

The first goal of the patriots was School Street and the home of Richard Clarke and his sons, Richard Clarke, Jr., and Jonathan Clarke. They called at the Clarkes's at one in the morning of November 2, 1773. A letter was given the family, demanding that the Clarkes appear at Liberty Tree, then at the site of today's Washington and Essex Streets, a central meeting place, at noon the following day.

Early the appointed morning a large flag was displayed from a pole on the Liberty Tree, while the town crier, bell in hand, went through the streets calling on all inhabitants to be present at noon that day. The people turned out in great numbers, but not one of the consignees of tea appeared.

On November 17 a crowd visited the Clarke mansion on School Street, during which time someone in the house discharged a pistol and the crowd answered with a great number of stones. Soon afterward the consignees and the officers of customs fled across the harbor to Castle William, which was then occupied by British troops.

On Sunday, November 28, the first of the four tea ships, the *Dartmouth,* docked with 114 chests of tea. On December 1, Captain James Bruce arrived with the *Eleanor* and more tea, while Captain Hezekiah Coffin and the brig *Beaver* soon followed with the remainder of the tea which Boston was to receive at that time. The fourth vessel, the *William,* also loaded with tea for New England, was destined never to reach Boston, as it was wrecked on Cape Cod.

The three tea craft were now tied up at Griffin's Wharf,

*Other tea ships also left England: the *London* started for Charlestown, the *Polly* for Philadelphia, and still later the *Nancy* would begin her trip to New York.

whose present-day location is several hundred yards inland, at the corner of Pearl Street and Atlantic Avenue, Boston. The captains were warned by the committee not to land any tea.

After promising to help the patriots, Captain Rotch of the *Dartmouth* changed his mind and stated that he could not possibly comply with the resolutions because they would ruin him financially.

A special meeting was called for December 11, 1773, at two o'clock in the afternoon. Harrassed Captain Rotch appeared at the meeting by request, after which he went to the customs officer with a committee, asking for a clearance so that the *Dartmouth* could sail. The customs officer refused, suggesting that later in the week his departure was possible, but not probable.

Finally December 16, 1773, arrived. The largest popular meeting in Boston up to that time convened at the Old South Meeting House which was crowded to its utmost capacity. Samuel Phillips Savage, having come in from Weston, was chosen moderator, while no less than two thousand out-of-towners were in the hall from various parts of New England.

When Captain Rotch was called to report, he stated that the collector would not grant him clearance for his tea ship *Dartmouth*. He was ordered at his peril to prepare the ship immediately for sea. Then he was to go out to the governor's residence in Milton, where Governor Hutchinson had gone to be relatively inaccessible, and demand a permit to pass the castle and enter the open sea. The meeting was adjourned until Captain Rotch could drive to Milton and return, but the people did not leave the assembly hall. It was about this time that John Rowe asked the question, "Who knows how tea will mingle with salt water?"

The assemblage waited, and the minutes passed. Josiah Quincy, Jr., took the occasion to discourse most ably on the affairs of the colonies, and was still talking when the meeting was brought to sharp attention by the return of Captain Rotch at 5:45 P.M. The crisis was at hand.

Governor Hutchinson had been forced to make a vital decision. He told Rotch he could send a company of soldiers to Griffin's Wharf to protect the tea, but that this act might bring on another Boston Massacre. He chose instead to send a message by Captain Rotch which was read to the meeting: "For the honor of the laws, and from duty toward the King, [he] could not grant the permit until the vessel was regularly cleared."

On hearing the governor's message, Samuel Adams leaped to his feet and shouted, "This meeting can do nothing more to save the country!"

This was what the assembly was waiting to hear, and Adams' outburst was the turning point of the entire situation. Up to that moment the people had been relatively passive, but from then on they would be active and aggressive.

The moment the reading ended, a person way up in the gallery, disguised "as an Indian, uttered a cry in imitation of the war-whoop," a cry which was answered at once by about thirty persons gathered at the doors in similar attire.

By prearrangement, the band of so-called Indians headed for the waterfront that night, proceeding on Milk Street, turning at Hutchinson Street, and continuing down to Cow Lane, where the masts and spars of the three tea craft were in sight. By the time the wharf was reached, there were no less than one hundred persons in the crowd, some dressed as Indians, some in ordinary garb.

Members of the Boston Tea Party boarded the *Dartmouth* first, and soon afterward another group started on the *Eleanor.* The tea on the *Beaver* was the last to be handled. In each case the officers and crew of the tea vessels were told what was to happen and ordered to keep out of the way. Then the tea chests were brought up on deck and broken open, and the tea was thrown over the side of the ship down onto the low tide flats.

The leaders were very orderly in carrying out their plans even to the extent of replacing a padlock which they had damaged on one of the tea ships. Down under the wharf boys had gathered for the purpose of crushing the tea into the mud flats, but by the time the ships were emptied, they "found their return upon deck much facilitated by the immense pile of tea, which had accumulated beneath and around them," and they walked right aboard on the tea.

Three of the lads were Henry Purkitt, Samuel Sprague, and John Hooten, all apprentices. They quickly went to work trampling the tea into the flats. When Purkitt arrived home, his feet were wet and muddy, and his clothing and shoes full of tea. A considerable portion of this tea was put away in a bottle and placed in a cupboard as a memento of the occasion. At the time of the one hundredth anniversary of the raid in 1873, the bottle was brought out by the person to whom it had been handed down and was displayed in Boston. Eventually, seventy years later, it would find its way to me. Other participants in the Tea Party also found tea in their shoes, as small vials now in both the Old State House and the Massachusetts Historical Society will attest.

After every single chest of tea on the three ships had been spilled overboard, the so-called Mohawk Indians went home with the others in the crowd in orderly fashion. The entire incident of the Tea Party lasted three hours, from about six to nine o'clock.

One partly smashed half chest floated ashore at what is now City Point, where it was found the next morning by Ebenezer Withington, who took it to his home near Sodom, in the vicinity of the Dorchester Meeting House. A committee visited the house, took the tea and publicly burned it on Boston Common.

On December 17, the morning after the party, a long windrow of tea, "about as big as you ever saw of hay," was seen extending all the way down Boston Harbor from the wharves to Castle Island. The consignees who were gathered there evidently realized what had happened at Griffin's Wharf the preceeding night.

A short time before, on December 10, the fourth craft loaded with tea for Boston Harbor had been wrecked at Provincetown, Cape Cod. Captain Loring's brigantine *William*, listed as carrying fifty-eight full chests of tea which occupied 585 square feet of cargo space, crashed on shore during a hurricane. All but two chests were taken off the *William* safely.

John Greenough, a Harvard College graduate who became a Wellfleet schoolteacher, took over the cargo, notifying the Clarkes in Boston, who sent two small vessels across Massachusetts Bay to Cape Cod Harbor at Provincetown where most of the salvaged tea was loaded aboard.

Sailing up to Castle Island in Boston Harbor with the tea, Greenough went ashore and told the Clarkes that there were two damaged chests back at Cape Cod which he felt he should be allowed to have. He trusted that no duty would be charged on them, for then he could sell them without any unpatriotic qualms. The commissioners at Castle William granted Greenough his wish.

Several tea lovers purchased the forbidden luxury from Greenough and others and were looked upon as Tories. Eventually the matter was brought up in the Truro Town Meeting of February 28, 1774. A number of persons in town appeared who had "purchased small quantities of the East India Co.'s baneful Teas lately cast ashore at Provincetown . . . through ignorance and inadvertence . . . by the villainous example and artful persuading of some noted pretended friends of government, from the neighboring towns."

The tea was traced back to Greenough, and feeling ran high against him for almost ten months.

Although ostracized by the Cape Codders, Greenough not only was back in good standing by 1774 but made a public statement on December 19 claiming that he wished to be reconciled "again and to forget and forgive on both sides."

The people of Cape Cod eventually did "forget and forgive," for in 1778 Greenough was one of five appointed to the Safety Committee, and the next year he was one of three delegates to the County Convention at Barnstable.

The last tea ship to arrive in Boston during the excitement carried twenty-eight and a half chests. After docking at Griffin's Wharf, Boston, on March 7, 1774, the brig *Fortune* was moved nearer to Hubbard's Wharf where a second Boston Tea Party within a year occurred. Every particle of tea was destroyed. This episode, however, which took place at 7:30 in the evening, never received the publicity of the first Tea Party of December 16, 1773.

After the first Boston Tea Party, Paul Revere was called upon to ride to New York and Philadelphia and tell the townspeople there of the action of the patriots. He was received with great acclaim in both communities. On his return to Boston he told of how Governor Tryon of New York had ordered the tea ships sent back to England, and the Boston people were so pleased with the news that all of the bells in the town were rung.

Some people may wonder why those who participated in the Tea Party were reluctant to give their names, causing endless confusion in later years. The reason is easy to understand when one considers that had we lost the Revolution, those known participants would have been summarily hanged by the English. Even as late as the War of 1812, when the British captured and burned Washington, few of the Tea Party members were admitting their identification.

Another point of never-ending confusion is the location of the Tea Party. Without question, over ten thousand people annually visit the site of T Wharf* and go home happy but mistaken in their belief that it was from T Wharf that the tea was thrown into the harbor. Actually it was from Griffin's Wharf, located between South Station and Rowe's Wharf now, where the tablet is today.

Another item of interest to some is that the tablet at 470 Atlantic Avenue has a minor error. It mentions 342 chests of tea whereas the correct number was 340. You may call this quibbling, but many visitors view the tablet, and it should be correct. In 1962 I interviewed a member of the group which erected the marker, and he agreed to make the change. Nothing has ever been done about it.

The reader may wonder how Henry Purkitt's bottle of tea finally came into my possession. In 1943 Jefferson Haskell Parker was introduced to me by Francis Haskell, one of the early presidents of the Massachusetts Marine Historical League. Parker was then approaching a century in age, a goal he eventually missed by a few weeks. Parker told me that he had gone fishing at Boston Light before the Civil War and would like to have me take him out on one of the excursions which we held and still conduct every pleasant weekend.

That very year I took him out to the Light, but it was so rough we could not land. Going ashore at Great Brewster Island, a half mile away, we started walking out over the low tide bar which connects with Boston Light, but his strength failed, and I carried him piggyback style the rest of the distance.

We visited the light, and the keeper volunteered later to row us back to Great Brewster, a plan to which I readily agreed. On our return journey to Boston, Parker told me

*Named because of its shape.

some of his earlier career. Still a member of the Boston
Watch and Ward Society, he explained how he had been a
newspaper editor in 1873, when the one hundredth anniversary of the Boston Tea Party was observed.

Parker told how a descendant of Henry Purkitt, the boy
who had gone home that night in 1773 with tea in his clothing, had brought in a bottle of tea Purkitt's mother had sifted
out of his garments. Parker placed the bottle of tea on exhibition. Then the owner of the tea died suddenly, so Parker kept
it. He gave the bottle to me, and within a short interval of
time he also passed away.

As the tea had not rightly been his, I interviewed a descendant of Henry Purkitt, Henry Purkitt Kidder, concerning the ethics of the situation. We decided to have our own
tea party on each anniversary, drinking a little of the original
tea every time.

At the present time most of the remainder of the little
bottle of tea is preserved in the Needham Historical Society
in Needham, Massachusetts.

In 1961 a group from Jackson County, Oregon, paid $1.96
for their county's proportional share of the Boston Tea Party
cost back in 1773. I talked with Henry Purkitt Kidder about
it, and we decided that I should pay in full for the approximately one pound of tea which Mrs. Purkitt had collected
from the clothing of her son Henry after he returned from
the affair.

My accountants figured that my share, including principal
and interest from December 16, 1773, to December 16, 1961,
would be $49.56. I wrote a check for that amount and sent
it to Leslie Simons, Davison and Newman, who had owned
the tea. Then an inaccurate story appeared in a Greater
Boston newspaper stating that I had sent a check for
$4,964.55 for the tea instead of the actual $49.56 I had paid.
This error gave the incident more importance than it other-

wise would have received. Because of this a German educa-
tor, Miss Ursula Page, wrote for details of the story. I sent
her the check, which by this time had been cashed by the
British firm, and in 1970 a photograph of the check and the
story appeared in a German school book entitled *Britain and
America*.

On May 18, 1960, Mr. Ernest Henderson of the Sheraton
chain of hotels gave British Ambassador Harold Caccia a
dinner at which tea I had presented to Mr. Henderson was
brewed and drunk. He also presented Sir Harold with several
original pennies to cover the tax, but the British Ambassador
pointedly stated, in fun, of course, that the tax was quite a
few years late in coming.

Indeed, the Boston Tea Party was a historical event, for
without the Tea Party of 1773, it is doubtful if there would
have been a Lexington and Concord sixteen months later.
The words of Oliver Wendell Holmes shall end this chapter.

No! never such a draught was poured
   Since Hebe served with nectar
The bright Olympians and their Lord,
   Her over-kind protector:
No! ne'er was mingled such a draught,
   In palace, hall or arbor,
As freemen brewed, and tyrants quaffed,
   That night in Boston Harbor.
The waters in the rebel bay
   Have kept the tea-leaf savor;
Our old North-enders in their spray
   Still taste a Hyson flavor.
And Freedom's tea-cup still o'erflows,
   With ever-fresh libations,
To cheat of slumber all her foes.
   And cheer the wakening nations!

INDEX

Index